Party KNITS

Published 2018—IMM Lifestyle Books
www.IMMLifestyleBooks.com

IMM Lifestyle Books are distributed in the UK by
Grantham Book Service, Trent Road, Grantham,
Lincolnshire, NG31 7XQ.

In North America, IMM Lifestyle Books
are distributed by Fox Chapel Publishing,
903 Square Street, Mount Joy, PA 17552,
www.FoxChapelPublishing.com.

ISBN 978-1-5048-0103-4

Party Knits is a collection of new and previously
published material. Portions of this book have been
reproduced from *Party Knits* (978-1-84773-224-8).

The Cataloging-in-Publication Data is on file
with the Library of Congress.

We are always looking for talented authors. To
submit an idea, please send a brief inquiry to
acquisitions@foxchapelpublishing.com.

Printed in Singapore
10 9 8 7 6 5 4 3 2 1

This book has been published with the intent to
provide accurate and authoritative information in
regard to the subject matter within. While every
precaution has been taken in the preparation of
this book, the authors and publisher expressly
disclaim any responsibility for any errors,
omissions, or adverse effects arising from the use
or application of the information contained herein.

Shutterstock photo credits: Esin Deniz (1);
IrenaStar (2–3); grafvision (6); Happy Stock Photo
(7); Nagy Mariann (9); Nataliia Pyzhova (10);
Steve Mann (11 top left); Sandra van der Steen
(11 top right); Anastasia E Kozlova (11 middle,
back cover bottom); HP Productions (11 bottom
left); Natasha Breen (11 bottom right); Tracey
Helmboldt (13); Nor Gar (14 bottom left); Nadiia
Ishchenko (18 bottom right); Dja65 (23 right);
Kristina Iakushina (136); and Africa Studio (141).

Party KNITS

· · · · · · · · · · · · · · · · · · · ·

25 *Stylish Designs for Any Party*

Melody Griffiths
& Lesley Stanfield

IMM lifestyle books
Read. Learn. Do What You Love.

32

35

42

26

54

60

65

76

81

84

88

96

114

118

122

127

129

46

50

70

74

102

107

131

134

Contents

Introduction

This is a collection of simple, inspired ideas to set your imagination racing. Knitwear can be curvy, cozy, decorated, textured, classic, clinging, see-through, or sophisticated. It can flatter your best features and gloss over the areas you want to hide. It can signal your individuality, whether you want to dress up or dress down. Best of all, hand knitting gives you the opportunity to create unique, luxurious clothes.

Here you'll find everything you need for that special occasion. From simple accessories to stunning sweaters and jackets, there are 25 up-to-the-minute stylish fashion items all of which can be made using the basic knitting skills outlined in the clear and concise Getting Started section (see pages 12–23), which includes extra explanation to help with any less familiar techniques.

There are three style sections to explore. All include designs for extra special evenings and for those daytime occasions when you want something a little dressier—from sexy shapes and daring body-conscious garments to fashion knits in fancy yarns; from subtle beaded decoration to all-over sequins—there's something for every type of party.

Choose the style that enhances your look and make it in the color that suits you. Mix your makes with basic black or fabulous fabrics, pile on the jewelery, or leave them plain. And when you've invested the time and care in making these knits, you'll find that they are fashion classics that will last many years, precious possessions that you wear over and over again.

Equipment

All you need to create beautiful hand knits is some yarn, knitting needles, simple sewing equipment, and patience!

YARNS

The designs in this book feature classic and fashion yarns. Enjoy the feel of luxury mixes such as cashmere, alpaca, and silk; choose shimmering metallic, smooth cotton, or man-made fibers with fabulous furry textures. Each design has been created with the particular qualities of the chosen yarn in mind. Ideally, you should always use the yarn specified, although the choice of color is up to you. Fashion yarns and colors change with the seasons, so if you do need to find a substitute yarn, check that the fiber content, yarn type, texture, and number of meters in a ball match the original as closely as possible.

These are the yarns used in this book (Note: Some brands may be difficult to locate in stores or online. You may either substitute it with a different brand similar in fiber content, or do an online search; Ebay is an excellent source for such instances.):

- Debbie Bliss Alpaca Silk DK: 80% baby alpaca, 20% silk. 115 yds. (105 m) per 1¾ oz. (50 g) ball.
- Debbie Bliss Cathay: 50% cotton, 35% microfiber, 15% silk. 110 yds. (100 m) per 1¾ oz. (50 g) ball.
- Debbie Bliss Pure Silk: 100% silk. 137 yds. (125 m) per 1¾ oz. (50 g) hank.
- Elle True Blue DK: 100% cotton. 118 yds. (108 m) per 1¾ oz. (50 g) ball.
- Jaeger Fur: 47% wool, 47% kid mohair, 6% polyamide. 22 yds. (20 m) per 1¾ oz. (50 g) ball.
- Rowan Lurex Shimmer: 80% viscose, 20% polyester. 104 yds. (95 m) per 1 oz. (25 g) ball.
- Rowan Kid Silk Haze: 70% super kid mohair, 30% silk. 229 yds. (210 m) per 1 oz. (25 g) ball.
- Rowan RYC Cashsoft DK: 57% extra fine merino, 33% microfiber, 10% cashmere. 142 yds. (130 m) per 1¾ oz. (50 g) ball.
- Rowan RYC Soft Lux: 64% extra fine merino wool, 10% angora, 24% nylon, 2% metallic fiber. 137 yds. (125 m) per 1¾ oz. (50 g) ball.
- Sirdar Boa: 100% polyester. 102 yds. (93 m) per 1¾ oz. (50 g) ball.
- Sirdar Foxy: 100% polyester. 44 yds. (40 m) per 1¾ oz. (50 g) ball.
- Sirdar Pure Cotton 4ply: 100% cotton. 370 yds. (338 m) per 3½ oz. (100 g) ball.
- Sirdar Town and Country 4ply: 75% wool, 25% nylon. 224 yds. (205 m) per 1¾ oz. (50 g) ball.
- Sirdar Wash 'n' Wear 4ply: 55% acrylic, 45% nylon. 510 yds. (466 m) per 3½ oz. (100 g) ball.
- Sirdar Zanzibar: 86% nylon, 14% polyester. 137 yds. (125 m) per 1¾ oz. (50 g) ball.

NEEDLES

Pairs of straight needles are the type most often used but for some of the projects you will also need a circular needle, a set of double pointed needles, or a cable needle.

Experiment with different lengths of straight needles and try out needles made from bamboo, plastic, or wood as well as classic aluminum to find the type of needles that are most comfortable for you. Remember that circular needles can be used for flat knitting as well as working in the round.

The needle size given in the instructions is the size that the knitter used to get the tension given when the sample garment was made. This needle size should be treated only as a guide; the size you need to use is the size that gives you the correct tension. If you're going out to buy needles, it makes sense to get one or two sizes above and below the recommended size, this way you'll soon build up a collection.

ACCESSORIES

You'll need a tape measure to check your tension and garment measurements and scissors to cut the yarn. A stitch holder can be useful, but you can always improvise with a circular needle or a length of yarn. Markers help keep track of the rows when shaping, or the stitches when working pattern repeats. Use the

KNITTING NEEDLE CONVERSION CHART

Metric	American	British
2.00 mm	00	14
2.25 mm	1	13
2.75 mm	2	12
3.00 mm	2/3	11
3.25 mm	3	10
3.75 mm	5	9
4.00 mm	6	8
4.50 mm	7	7
5.00 mm	8	6
5.50 mm	8	5
6.00 mm	9	4
6.50 mm	10	3
7.00 mm	10½	2
7.50 mm	11	1
8.00 mm	12	0
9.00 mm	13	00
10.00 mm	15	000

plastic hook-on type, safety pins, or loops of smooth contrast yarn. A blunt-pointed wool needle is essential for sewing up, a sharp pointed needle will split the stitches. Largeheaded pins set at right angles to the seam keep the pieces in place when sewing up, especially when fitting a sleeve head into the armhole, and a slim tapestry needle will slip through the holes more easily when sewing on buttons.

BEADS AND SEQUINS

From scattered decoration to all-over coverage, even the simplest knits get the glamour treatment with added beads and sequins. Some of these designs have beads or sequins knitted in, others have the decoration sewn on after the knitting is finished. You can choose from lots of different types—glass, metallic, or plastic—and shapes of beads. Most of the round beads used in this book are rocaille or embroidery beads, often described as size 5 or 5/0, these can be sewn on or knitted in. Where you need a larger quantity of beads for knitting in, you'll find that buying beads

in packs of 10½ oz. (300 g) or 17½ oz. (500 g) works out cheaper than buying lots of small tubes, even if some beads are left over. Finer seed beads and bugle beads are only suitable for sewing on. Buying small packs makes sense as this will give you more choice. You could also recycle broken necklaces or use antique beads to give a vintage effect.

When buying beads or sequins, take a ball of the yarn along with you to be sure that they match or contrast with the color of the yarn and that, if necessary, the hole in the beads is big enough to thread them onto the yarn. Sequins are made in many different shapes and sizes, round flat, round cupped, square, or oval. Any type of sequin can be sewn on and it can often be effective to use several related shades in a design. The round, flat sequins for knitting in are usually sold in strands of 1,000. Check when you buy that they are on a thread not loose in a pack as this will make it a lot easier to thread them onto the yarn. If you are matching sequins and yarn, always choose a yarn color that is darker than the sequins; a lighter shade will dominate the sequin color.

Getting Started

FOLLOWING THE INSTRUCTIONS

Before you start to knit, read through the instructions to be sure that you understand the abbreviations and you can cope with all the techniques needed. Abbreviations are used for many of the repetitive words that occur in the instructions. See the box opposite for a list of the most frequently used abbreviations; any additional abbreviations are given with the instructions. Some abbreviations look complex but make sense once you realise that they explain a series of actions such as skpo for slip one stitch knitwise, knit one stitch, pass the slipped stitch over.

Square brackets are used to show how many times a series of stitches should be worked or to clarify working a group of stitches. Square brackets are also placed around stitch counts. Asterisks indicate where to repeat instructions from or which part of the instructions to work again.

Check that you know which measurements you are working to. The amount of movement room varies according to the design so if you are not sure which size to make, check the actual measurements given against an existing garment that fits you well.

Where instructions for different sizes are given, the smallest size is given first, followed by the other sizes in round brackets, separated by colons. If there is only one figure, it refers to all of the sizes.

ABBREVIATIONS	
beg	beginning
cont	continu(e)(ing)
dec	decreas(e)(ing)
foll	following
inc	increas(e)(ing)
k	knit
kfb	knit into front and back of stitch
m1	make a stitch by lifting strand between stitches and knitting into the back of it
p	purl
patt	pattern
rem	remaining
rep	repeat
RS	right side
sl	slip
skpo	slip one knitwise, knit one, pass slipped stitch over
st(s)	stitch(es)
st-st	stocking stitch
tbl	through back of loop(s)
tog	together
WS	wrong side
yo	yarn over needle to make a stitch

CHECKING YOUR TENSION

This is the job that everyone hates! But you really must make sure that your tension matches the tension given or your garment will not be the correct size. Start with the needle size given and knit a swatch in the stitch pattern given for the item. The instructions under tension tell you how many stitches and how many rows make a 4-in. (10-cm) square, but cast on slightly more stitches and work a few more rows than given as the edge stitches will distort. Count and mark the correct number of stitches and rows from the center of the swatch. If your marked stitches and rows measure less than they should your knitting is too tight and the garment will be too small, so try again using larger needles. If they measure more, your knitting is too loose and the garment will be too big, try again using smaller needles. It can be difficult to see the stitches in some textured yarns so try holding the swatch up to the light to count and mark the stitches and rows, then lay it flat to measure.

Here's a reminder of the essential knitting techniques.

MAKING A SLIP KNOT

A slip knot counts as the first stitch.

Leaving an end that's long enough to cast on the required number of stitches, make a loop in the yarn. Insert the tip of the right needle and pull a loop through. Gently pull on the yarn to tighten the knot and to close the loop on the needle.

CASTING ON

Knitting into a loop around the thumb to make a stitch on the needle is the easiest and most versatile method of casting on.

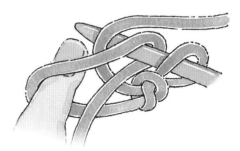

After making a slip knot, hold the needle and the yarn from the ball in the right or left hand. Using the long end, make a loop around left thumb, and insert right needle tip. Bring the yarn up between thumb and needle and take it around the needle.

Draw yarn through to make a stitch on the needle, release loop from left thumb and tighten the long end ready to make the next stitch.

MAKING A KNIT STITCH
(with yarn in right hand)

Hold the needle with the cast-on stitches in the left hand and the empty needle in the right hand. The yarn from the ball is at the back and is held in the right hand.

Bring right needle forward and taking it under left needle, insert it from left to right into front of first stitch, take the yarn up and around right needle.

With tip of right needle, draw a loop of yarn forward through the stitch on left needle, then drop stitch off left needle and tension yarn to make a stitch on right needle. Work into each stitch on the left needle in turn to complete a knit row.

MAKING A PURL STITCH
(with yarn in right hand)

Hold the needles in the same way as for making a knit stitch but bring the yarn from the ball to the front.

Taking right needle under left needle, insert it from right to left into front of first stitch, take yarn over and around right needle.

Dip the tip of the right needle away from you to draw a loop of yarn through stitch on left needle, then drop stitch off left needle and tension yarn to make a stitch on right needle. Work into each stitch on the left needle in turn to complete a purl row.

MAKING A KNIT STITCH
(with yarn in left hand)

Hold the needle with the cast-on stitches in the left hand and the empty needle in the right hand. The yarn from the ball is at the back and is held in the left hand, taut over the first finger.

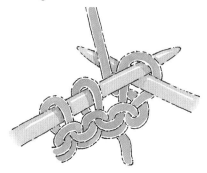

Bring the right needle forward and taking it under left needle, insert it from left to right into front of first stitch, then hook the right needle over and under the yarn.

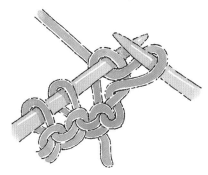

With tip of right needle, draw a loop of yarn forward and through the stitch on left needle, then drop stitch off left needle and tension the yarn to make a stitch on right needle. Work into each stitch in turn to complete a knit row.

MAKING A PURL STITCH
(with yarn in left hand)

Hold the needles in the same way as for a knit stitch but bring the yarn from the ball to the front and hold it in the left hand, taut over the first finger.

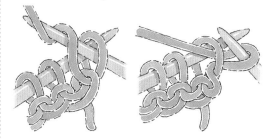

Taking right needle under left needle, insert it from right to left into first stitch, then hook the right needle over and under the yarn. Dip the tip of the right needle downward and away from you to draw a loop of yarn through stitch on left needle, then drop stitch off left needle and tension the yarn to make a stitch on right needle. Work into each stitch on the left needle in turn to complete a purl row.

CASTING OFF

Lifting one stitch over the next secures the stitches and makes a neat edge. Working every stitch as a knit stitch will give a chain edge, casting off in purl will give a nubbly edge.

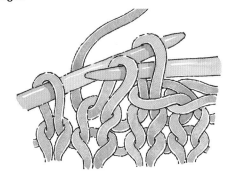

Knit two stitches. Use the point of the left needle to lift the first stitch over the second stitch and off the needle. Knit the next stitch so there are two stitches on right needle. Lift one stitch over and off right needle. Continue until there is one stitch left on right needle. Break yarn, draw end through, and pull it tight to secure the last stitch.

Special Techniques

This section leads you through a variety of ways to manipulate stitches to create everything from the subtlest shaping to delicate lace stitches or rich surface textures.

INCREASING

Simple increases make one stitch. The first method makes a little bar at the base of the new stitch, the second is almost invisible, and the third makes a decorative hole. More complex increases make two or more stitches integrated with the shaping or patterning.

Single increase: kfb

Knitting into the front and back of a stitch makes two stitches from one.

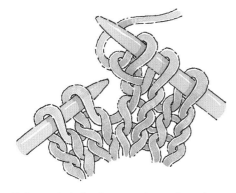

Knit a stitch in the usual way but do not allow stitch to drop off left needle, take right needle tip behind left needle to knit into the back of the same stitch, then drop stitch off left needle.

Single increase: m1

Working into the strand lying between stitches is a neat way to increase one stitch. Make sure that the strand crosses over at the base of the new stitch or you'll make a hole in the work.

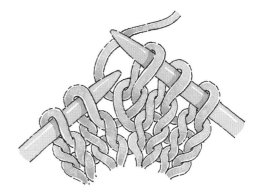

Bring left needle forward and inserting tip from front to back of work, lift the strand from between the needles. Take right needle behind to knit into back of strand. If you want the strand to cross over in the opposite direction, place the strand on the left needle in the opposite direction and work into the front of it. This type of increase can also be worked as a purl stitch, lift the strand in the same way, then purl into the back of it.

Single increase: yo

Taking the yarn around the needle makes a stitch with a decorative hole at the base. Larger holes can be made by working more yarn-overs.

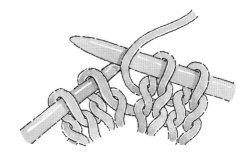

Between two knit stitches, bring the yarn between the needles to the front of the work and over the needle ready to knit the next stitch.

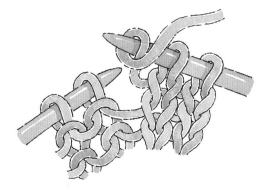

Between a knit and a purl stitch, bring the yarn to the front, over the needle and to the front again ready to purl the next stitch.

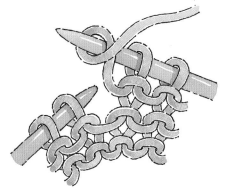

Between a purl and a purl, take the yarn over the needle and to the front again ready to purl the next stitch.

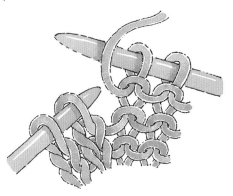

Between a purl and a knit stitch, the yarn is already at the front of the work, take it over the needle ready to knit the next stitch. Work this yarn over loosely or it will appear to be smaller than the other types of yarn over.

Double increase: d inc
This method makes three stitches from one stitch, almost invisibly.

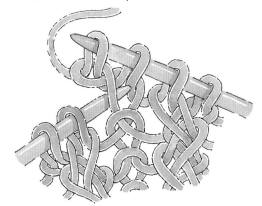

Knit in to the back and front of the stitch, then insert left needle tip behind the vertical strand that runs downward from between the two stitches just made and knit in to the back of this strand.

DECREASING

Simple decreases take two stitches together to make one stitch. The first two methods are mirror images usually worked in pairs to give a fully-fashioned effect. More complex two-stitch decreases can be used for both shaping and patterning.

Single decrease: k2tog

Knitting two stitches together is the easiest way to decrease one stitch. The second stitch lies on top and the decrease slants to the right.

Insert right needle through the fronts of the next two stitches on left needle, then knit the stitch in the usual way, slipping both stitches off left needle together.

Single decrease: skpo

Slip one stitch knitwise, knit one stitch, pass the slipped stitch over to make the mirror image of k2tog. The first stitch lies on top and the decrease slants to the left.

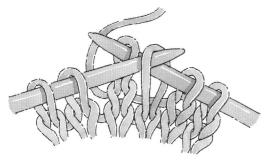

Slip the first stitch, knit the next stitch, use the tip of the left needle to lift the slipped stitch over and off the right needle.

Double decrease: sk2po

Slip one, knit two together, pass the slipped stitch over is the easiest way to take three stitches together. The first stitch lies on top, the third stitch is next, and the second stitch is at the back, the decrease slants to the left.

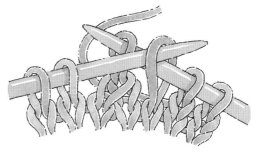

Slip the first stitch, knit the next two stitches together, then use the tip of the left needle to lift the slipped stitch over and off the right needle.

Double decrease: s2kpo

Slip two stitches, knit one, pass the slipped stitches over is another way to take three stitches together. The center stitch lies on top.

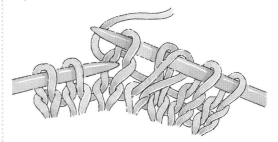

Insert right needle through the fronts of the first two stitches on left needle as if to knit two together, then slip these stitches onto right needle, knit the next stitch, use the tip of the left needle to lift the two slipped stitches over and off the right needle.

CABLES

Cable stitch patterns are made by using a short double-pointed needle to change the place of two or more stitches in a row. Cables can be worked with knit stitches only or with a combination of knit and purl stitches.

Cable back: c4b

This cable slants to the right.

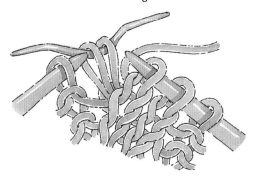

Slip the next two stitches onto a cable needle, hold the cable needle at the back of the work, knit the next two stitches on the left needle, then knit the two stitches from the cable needle and continue the row.

Cable front: c4f

This cable slants to the left.

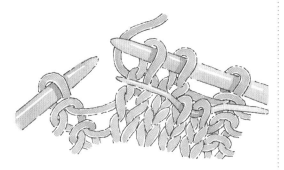

Slip the next two stitches on to a cable needle, hold the cable needle at the front of the work, knit the next two stitches on the left needle, then knit the two stitches from the cable needle and continue the row.

TWISTS

Twist stitch patterns are made by knitting or purling the stitches in a different order.

Knit twist: t2k

This method twists two stitches knitwise on right side rows.

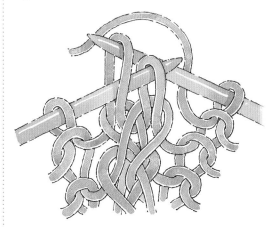

Take needle behind first stitch on left-hand needle and knit in to the back of the second stitch, bring the needle forward and knit in to the front of the first stitch, slip both stitches off left needle together.

Purl twist: t2p

This twists two stitches purlwise on wrong side rows.

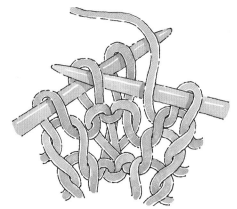

Take needle in front of first stitch on left-hand needle to purl the second stitch, then purl the first stitch and slip both stitches off left needle together.

LOOP STITCH

This method of making a single loop is very stable, it won't stretch or slip back and open up the fabric.

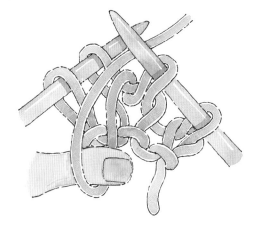

Knit the stitch in the usual way but do not allow it to drop off left needle; bring the yarn to the front between the needles, take it under then over left thumb and back between the needles; knit the stitch on left needle again and slip it off in the usual way, then lift the previous stitch on the right needle over it.

Decorative Effects

Beads and sequins can be knitted in or sewn on. For all-over beads and sequins, thread them on to the yarn before starting to knit. If the yarn is fine you may be able to thread directly on to the yarn with a fine needle, if not, then use the method here. When sewing on beads and sequins, match the thread as closely as possible and use a small, sharp-pointed needle.

THREADING BEADS OR SEQUINS

Using an intermediary loop of thread makes it easier to slip the beads or sequins on to the yarn.

Thread a fine needle with a short length of strong sewing thread, knot the ends together, and slide the knot to the side. Pass the end of the yarn through the loop of thread. Pick up the beads or groups of sequins onto the needle, slide them over the loop of thread, and down onto the yarn.

KNITTING IN BEADS

The simplest way of knitting with beads is to work them between stitches.

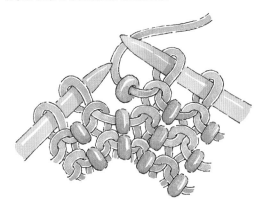

Work until ready to place a bead, bring a bead up close to the knitting, then work the next stitch so the bead hangs between the stitches. This can be done on knit or purl rows but the beads show up more between purl stitches.

SEWING ON BEADS

Using backstitch anchors beads firmly.

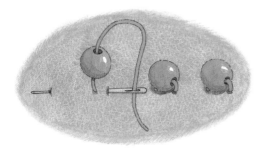

Bring the needle out where the bead is to be positioned, take the needle through the bead and, holding the bead close to the work, insert the needle just behind the bead ready to be brought out where the next bead is required.

KNITTING IN SEQUINS

Sequin knitting is basically just stocking stitch. Bringing a sequin through to the right side of the work as you knit a stitch makes the sequin lie flat on the front of knitting. Working the stitch through the back of the loop is not necessary for all yarns but will help stop the sequin slipping through to the wrong side when working with a smooth yarn.

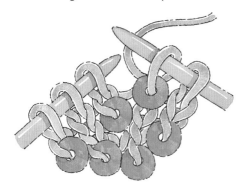

Work until ready to place a sequin, insert the left needle into the back of the next stitch, bring a sequin up close to the work, and slip the sequin through to the right side as you knit the stitch.

SEWING ON SEQUINS

Sequins can be sewn on with backstitch in the same way as beads but holding the sequin in place with a seed bead gives a decorative effect that hides the sewing yarn and the hole in the sequin.

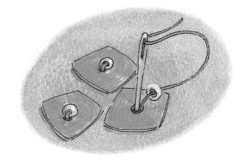

Place the sequin. Bring the needle up through the hole in the center of the sequin, then slide a bead on to the needle and down the thread. Take the needle around the bead and back down the hole. Tension the thread to bring the bead close to the sequin and secure the thread on the wrong side with a few backstitches before moving on to the next sequin.

Finishing

Each set of instructions explains the best way to put the knitting together but here are some general points about making up knits.

PRESSING

Blocking the pieces by pinning them out to shape and steam pressing on the wrong side before making up gives a professional finish especially for garments in natural fibers. Press the seams as you construct the garment.

Always check the yarn care instructions on the ball band because yarns in man-made fibers often cannot be pressed, in which case they can be pinned out to size, sprayed lightly with water, and left to dry to set the shapes before sewing up. Beaded knits can be pressed on the wrong side, using a cloth to protect the surface but garments covered in sequins should never be pressed.

SEWING UP

The best way to sew seams in knitting is to work with the right side facing so you can match stitches or row-ends to give an almost invisible join. Using the tail of yarn left over from casting on or casting off makes a neat start. To join a new length of yarn, simply run the needle through a few edge stitches before bringing the needle up to continue stitching. When the sewing up is complete, darn in ends from joining new balls of yarn along the seams, not along the rows.

MATTRESS STITCH

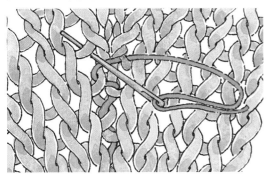

Use this to join side and sleeve seams. Working from side to side alternately, insert needle under the strand between stitches, one stitch in from the edge. Every two or three stitches, tension the yarn to bring the edges together.

Garment Care

Look after your hand-knits and they will last a long time. Store knits folded flat, if placed on a hanger they will drop. Products with essential oils and Neem are good natural moth deterrents but the best way to keep moths at bay is to make sure that your knits are scrupulously clean before you put them away.

Before washing garments, always remember to turn them inside out. Garments without decoration can be washed according to the yarn manufacturer's instructions. Decorated garments should be washed by hand, checking first that any beads are colorfast. Dry garments flat wherever possible.

Some types of beads should not be washed, check the appropriate care when you buy them.

Jewel Colors

Stand out from the crowd in striking shades of ruby red, sapphire blue, hot pink, lime green, magenta, and purple or go for the subtle approach with opal green and rose-quartz pink. Choose a brief camisole or a cover-up cardigan coat in the softest pastel shades. Slip into sexy shapes in classic yarns with an off-the-shoulder top and a dramatic V-back slimline sweater or revel in vibrant tones and textures with a skimpy shrug in fine mohair, a frill edge bolero, a fur coat, and a velvet-effect jacket. Finally, accent your look with a bright beaded bag or a fun flower corsage.

The yarn is so thick that you need very few stitches to create this fabulously furry coat. It's just the right length to wear over trousers or with more formal evening clothes.

Fun Furry Coat

EASY

MEASUREMENTS

To fit bust

in.	34–36	38–40	42–44	46–48
cm	86–91	97–102	107–112	117–122

Actual bust

in.	39½	43½	47¼	51¼
cm	100	110	120	130

Actual length

in.	39	40	41	41¾
cm	99.5	102	104	106.5

Actual sleeve length

in.	20
cm	51

In the instructions, figures are given for the smallest size first; larger sizes follow in brackets. Where only one figure is given, this applies to all sizes.

MATERIALS

- 22 (24: 26: 28) × 1¾ oz. (50 g) balls of Jaeger Fur in Fox, 054
- Pair of size 15 (10 mm) knitting needles
- Kilt pin or brooch

TENSION

- 8 sts and 9 rows to 4 in. (10 cm) over st-st on size 15 (10 mm) needles. Change needle size if necessary to obtain this tension.

ABBREVIATIONS

- [ ] – work instructions in square brackets as directed

See also page 12.

NOTES

- Actual bust measurement is calculated with seam stitches taken off and fronts wrapped over.
- When knitted, Fur is so textured it is quite hard to see the stitches and rows. To check your tension, cast on 10 sts, st-st 11 rows and cast off. Place markers one stitch in from each edge and one row in from cast-on and cast-off edges, measure each way. If you get less than 4 in. (10 cm) try again using larger needles, if you get more than 4 in. (10 cm), try again using smaller needles.
- Shapings are given on knit rows as this is easier to work but make up the coat with the reverse side of stocking stitch as the right side to show the furry texture.

- Take the yarn end from the center of the ball, it will stop the ball rolling around and picking up bits as you knit.
- Place markers at each end of shaping rows on back and sleeves and at side edges on fronts to help to keep track of the rows between increases or decreases.
- Join seams with the right side facing, using mattress stitch. Match and remove the markers as you sew up.

BACK

Cast on 56 (60: 64: 68) sts.

Beg k row, st-st until back measures 4¼ in. (11 cm), ending with a p row.

1st dec row: (WS) K1, k2tog, k15 (16: 17: 18), k2tog, k16 (18: 20: 22), skpo, k15 (16: 17: 18), skpo, k1. [52 (56: 60: 64) sts.]

St-st 9 rows.

2nd dec row: (WS) K1, k2tog, k13 (14: 15: 16), k2tog, k16 (18: 20: 22), skpo, k13 (14: 15: 16), skpo, k1. [48 (52: 56: 60) sts.]

St-st 9 rows.

3rd dec row: (WS) K1, k2tog, k11 (12: 13: 14), k2tog, k16 (18: 20: 22), skpo, k11 (12: 13: 14), skpo, k1. [44 (48: 52: 56) sts.]

St-st 7 rows.

4th dec row: (WS) K1, k2tog, k9 (10: 11: 12), k2tog, k16 (18: 20: 22), skpo, k9 (10: 11: 12), skpo, k1. [40 (44: 48: 52) sts.]

St-st 5 rows.

5th dec row: (WS) K1, k2tog, k7 (8: 9: 10), k2tog, k16 (18: 20: 22), skpo, k7 (8: 9: 10), skpo, k1. [36 (40: 44: 48) sts.]

St-st 7 rows.

Inc row: (WS) Kfb, k to last 2 sts, kfb, k1.

Cont in st-st, inc in this way at each end of 2 foll 4th rows. [42 (46: 50: 54) sts.]

St-st 5 rows.

Shape Armholes

Cast off 2 sts at beg of next 2 rows.

Dec row: (WS) K1, k2tog, k to last 3 sts, skpo, k1.

Cont in st-st, dec in this way at each end of next 2 (3: 4: 5) WS rows. [32 (34: 36: 38) sts.]

St-st 17 rows. Cast off.

RIGHT FRONT

Cast on 31 (33: 35: 37) sts.

Beg k row, st-st until front measures 4¼ in. (11 cm), ending with a p row.

1st dec row: (WS) K1, k2tog, k15 (16: 17: 18), k2tog, k11 (12: 13: 14). [29 (31: 33: 35) sts.]

St-st 9 rows.

2nd dec row: (WS) K1, k2tog, k13 (14: 15: 16), k2tog, k11 (12: 13: 14). [27 (29: 31: 33) sts.]

St-st 9 rows.

3rd dec row: (WS) K1, k2tog, k11 (12: 13: 14), k2tog, k11 (12: 13: 14). [25 (27: 29: 31) sts.]

St-st 7 rows.

4th dec row: (WS) K1, k2tog, k9 (10: 11: 12), k2tog, k11 (12: 13: 14). [23 (25: 27: 29) sts.]

St-st 5 rows.

5th dec row: (WS) K1, k2tog, k7 (8: 9: 10), k2tog, k11 (12: 13: 14). [21 (23: 25: 27) sts.]

St-st 7 rows.

Inc row: (RS) Kfb, k to end. Cont in st-st, inc in this way at beg of 2 foll 4th rows. [24 (26: 28: 30) sts.]

St-st 5 rows.

Shape Armhole

Cast off 2 sts at beg of next row. P 1 row.

Dec row: (WS) K1, k2tog, k to end.

Cont in st-st, dec in this way at beg of next 2 (3: 4: 5) RS rows. [19 (20: 21: 22) sts.]

St-st 5 rows.

Shape Collar

Inc row: (RS) K to last 2 sts, kfb, k1.

Cont in st-st, inc in this way at end of next 3 WS rows. [23 (24: 25: 26) sts.] P 1 row.

- If your tension is just a little bit off, try holding the yarn more tightly or more loosely, rather than changing needle size.
- If you don't want to pin the fronts, buy matching ribbon and make ties.

Shape Neck

1st row: (WS) K11 (12: 13: 14), cast off 12.
2nd row: (RS) Join yarn, p2tog, p to end.
3rd row: K to last 2 sts, skpo.
4th row: P2tog, p to end. [8 (9: 10: 11) sts.]
  Cast off.

LEFT FRONT

Cast on 31 (33: 35: 37) sts.
Beg k row, st-st until front measures 4¼ in.
  (11 cm), ending with a p row.
1st dec row: (WS) K11 (12: 13: 14), skpo, k15
  (16: 17: 18), skpo, k1. [29 (31: 33: 35) sts.]
St-st 9 rows.
2nd dec row: (WS) K11 (12: 13: 14), skpo, k13
  (14: 15: 16), skpo, k1. [27 (29: 31: 33) sts.]
St-st 9 rows.
3rd dec row: (WS) K11 (12: 13: 14), skpo, k11
  (12: 13: 14), skpo, k1. [25 (27: 29: 31) sts.]
St-st 7 rows.
4th dec row: (WS) K11 (12: 13: 14), skpo, k9
  (10: 11: 12), skpo, k1. [23 (25: 27: 29) sts.]
St-st 5 rows.
5th dec row: (WS) K11 (12: 13: 14), skpo, k7 (8:
  9: 10), skpo, k1. [21 (23: 25: 27) sts.]
St-st 7 rows.
Inc row: (WS) K to last 2 sts, kfb, k1.
Cont in st-st, inc in this way at end of 2 foll
  4th rows. [24 (26: 28: 30) sts.] St-st 6 rows.

Shape Armhole

Cast off 2 sts at beg of next row.
Dec row: (WS) K to last 3 sts, skpo, k1.
Cont in st-st, dec in this way at end of next 2
  (3: 4: 5) WS rows. [19 (20: 21: 22) sts.]
St-st 5 rows.

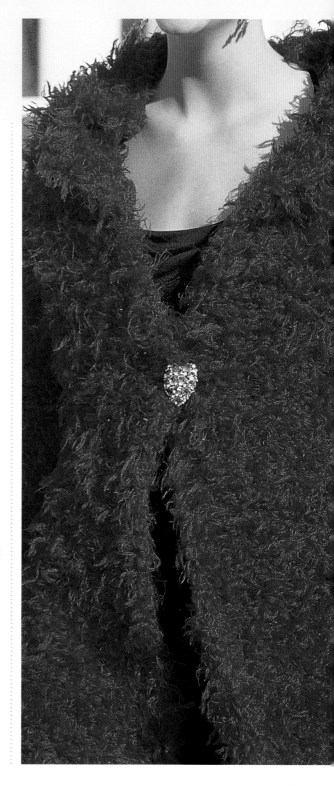

Shape Collar

Inc row: (WS) Kfb, k to end.

Cont in st-st, inc in this way at beg of next 3 WS rows. [23 (24: 25: 26) sts.] P1 row.

Shape Neck

1st row: (WS) Cast off 12 sts, k to end. [11 (12: 13: 14) sts.]

2nd row: P to last 2 sts, p2tog.

3rd row: K2tog, k to end.

4th row: P to last 2 sts, p2tog. [8 (9: 10: 11) sts.]

Cast off.

SLEEVES

Cast on 20 (22: 24: 26) sts. Beg k row, st-st until sleeve measures 5 in. (13 cm), ending with a p row.

Inc row: (WS) Kfb, k to last 2 sts, kfb, k1. Cont in st-st, inc in this way at each end of 4 foll 6th rows. [30 (32: 34: 36) sts.]

St-st until sleeve measures 20 in. (51 cm), ending with a p row.

Shape Top

Cast off 2 sts at beg of next 2 rows.

Dec row: (WS) K1, k2tog, k to last 3 sts, skpo, k1.

Cont in st-st, dec in this way at each end of next 2 (3: 4: 5) WS rows. [20 sts.] P 1 row.

Next row: (WS) Slipping first st, cast off 2 sts, k to last 2 sts, skpo. [17 sts.]

Next row: Slipping first st, cast off 2 sts, p to last 2 sts, p2tog. [14 sts.]

Work last 2 rows again. [8 sts.] Cast off.

COLLAR

Matching sts, join shoulders. With WS facing, beg at 6th st from front edge of left front collar, k up 13 sts up left front neck, 16 sts across back neck, and 13 sts down right front neck, ending at 6th st from front edge. [42 sts.] Beg p row, st-st 8 rows. Cast off.

TO MAKE UP

Set in sleeves. Join side and sleeve seams, reversing seam for turn-back cuff if wished.

Choose vibrant reds or soft pinks for this light-hearted woolly flower decoration.

Rose Corsage

EASY

MEASUREMENTS
o The flower is approximately 2¼ in. (7 cm) across.

MATERIALS
o Oddments of DK yarn in shades of pink and green
o Pair of size 5 (3.75 mm) knitting needles
o Small safety pin

ABBREVIATIONS
See page 12.

CENTER PETALS (make 3)
With deep pink, cast on 3 sts.
1st row: Kfb twice, k1. [5 sts.]
2nd row: K.
3rd row: Kfb, k2, kfb, k1. [7 sts.]
4th row: K.
5th row: Kfb, k4, kfb, k1. [9 sts.]
6th row: K.
7th row: K1, [k2tog] 4 times. [5 sts.]
8th row: K.
9th row: K1, [k2tog] twice. [3 sts.]
10th row: K.
Break yarn and leave sts on a spare needle.
Leave second and third petals on same needle.

OUTER PETALS (make 5)
With paler pink, cast on 5 sts.
1st row: Kfb 4 times, k1. [9 sts.]
2nd row: K.
3rd row: Kfb, k6, kfb, k1. [11 sts.]
4th–8th rows: K.
9th row: K1, [k2tog] 5 times. [6 sts.]
10th row: K.
11th row: K1, [k2tog] twice, k1. [4 sts.]
12th row: K.

○ Making petals and leaves requires some careful darning in of ends but the rose is really very easy to knit.

Darn in remaining petal ends.
Coil into a ring, alternating petals as far as possible, then use long end to secure by stitching base.
To hold petals in half-open position, use paler pink to stitch outer petals to each other at a point about halfway up the petal.

LEAVES (make 3)
With green, cast on 10 sts.
1st row: Kfb, k7, k2tog.
2nd row: K.
Repeat these 2 rows 4 times more, then work 1st row again.
Cast off knitwise.
Make second piece the same, then stitch both pieces together around the edges.

TO MAKE UP
Attach leaves to rose. Stitch safety pin to underside.

Break yarn and leave sts on a spare needle.
Leave second, third, fourth, and fifth petals on same needle.

BASE
Darn in cast-on ends of yarn on each petal.
With deep pink, k sts of each petal in turn, starting with 5 outer petals and ending with 3 center petals. [29 sts.]
K 2 rows.
Cast off, working k2tog to last st, k 1. Break yarn, leaving an end long enough to sew with.

Soft alpaca silk-mix yarn makes a floppy fabric with a subtle sheen for this easy-to-wear top.

Frill Edge Vest

ADVANCED

MEASUREMENTS

To fit bust

in.	32	34	36	38	40	42
cm	81	86	91	97	102	107

Actual bust

in.	33	35½	37½	39¾	41¾	44
cm	84	90	95	101	106	112

Actual length

in.	24	24¼	24¾	25¼	25½	26
cm	61	61.5	63	64	65	66.5

In the instructions, figures are given for the smallest size first; larger sizes follow in brackets. Where only one figure is given, this applies to all sizes.

MATERIALS

- 7 (8: 8: 9: 10: 11) × 1¾ oz. (50 g) balls of Debbie Bliss Alpaca Silk DK in magenta, 007
- Pair of size 6 (4 mm) knitting needles
- Size 6 (4 mm) circular needles, 39½ in. (100 cm) and 15¾ in. (40 cm) long
- 2¼ yd. (2 m) stretch lace for tie

TENSION

- 20 sts and 28 rows to 4 in. (10 cm) over lace patt, 22 sts and 28 rows to 4 in. (10 cm) over st-st, both on size 6 (4 mm) needles. Change needle size if necessary to obtain these tensions.

ABBREVIATIONS

- **m1k** – lift strand between sts and k into back of it
- **m1p** – lift strand between sts and p into back of it
- **sk2po** – slip one knitwise, k2tog, pass slipped st over
- **[ ]** – work instructions in square brackets as directed

See also page 12.

BACK

Cast on 82 (86: 92: 98: 104: 110) sts.

1st row: (RS) K4 (6: 9: 12: 15: 18), [yo, p2tog, k7] 8 times, yo, p2tog, k4 (6: 9: 12: 15: 18).

2nd, 4th, and 6th rows: P4 (6: 9: 12: 15: 18), [yo, p2tog, p7] 8 times, yo, p2tog, p4 (6: 9: 12: 15: 18).

3rd row: K4 (6: 9: 12: 15: 18), [yo, p2tog, k3, yo, k2tog, k2] 8 times, yo, p2tog, k4 (6: 9: 12: 15: 18).

5th row: K4 (6: 9: 12: 15: 18), * yo, p2tog, k2, [yo, k2tog] twice, k1, rep from * 7 more times, yo, p2tog, k4 (6: 9: 12: 15: 18).

These 6 rows form lace patt with st-st at each side. Patt 6 more rows.

Dec row: (RS) K2, k2tog, patt to last 4 sts, skpo, k2.

1st size only: Cont in patt, work 29 rows.

All other sizes: Cont in patt, dec in this way at each end of 2 foll 10th rows. Patt 9 rows.

All sizes: [80 (80: 86: 92: 98: 104) sts.]

Inc row: (RS) K1, kfb, patt to last 3 sts, kfb, k2.

Cont in patt, inc in this way at each end of 2 (5: 5: 5: 5: 5) foll 6th rows. [86 (92: 98: 104: 110: 116) sts.]

Patt 35 (17: 17: 17: 17: 17) rows.

Shape Armholes

Cast off 3 (4: 4: 5: 6: 6) sts at beg of next 2 rows.

3rd row: (RS) Skpo, patt to last 2 sts, k2tog.

Cont in patt, dec in this way at each end of next 3 (5: 5: 6: 7: 9) RS rows. [72 (72: 78: 80: 82: 84) sts.]

Cont in patt, work 47 (45: 49: 49: 51: 51) rows. Cast off.

LEFT FRONT

Cast on 25 (27: 30: 33: 36: 39) sts.

1st row: (RS) K4 (6: 9: 12: 15: 18), [yo, p2tog, k7] twice, yo, p2tog, m1k, k1.

2nd row: P1, m1p, p1, [yo, p2tog, p7] twice, yo, p2tog, p4 (6: 9: 12: 15: 18).

3rd row: K4 (6: 9: 12: 15: 18), [yo, p2tog, k3, yo, k2tog, k2] twice, yo, p2tog, k2, m1k, k1.

4th row: P1, m1p, p3, [yo, p2tog, p7] twice, yo, p2tog, p4 (6: 9: 12: 15: 18).

5th row: K4 (6: 9: 12: 15: 18), * yo, p2tog, k2, [yo, k2tog] twice, k1, rep from * once more, yo, p2tog, k4, m1k, k1.

6th row: P1, m1p, p5, [yo, p2tog, p7] twice, yo, p2tog, p4 (6: 9: 12: 15: 18). [31 (33: 36: 39: 42: 45) sts.]

These 6 rows set patt to match back with incs at front edge.

7th row: Patt to last 7 sts, k6, m1k, k1.

8th row: P1, m1p, p7, patt to end.

9th row: Patt to last 9 sts, k3, yo, k2tog, k2, yo, p1, k1.

10th row: P1, m1p, yo, p2tog, patt to end.

11th row: Patt to last 2 sts, k1, m1k, k1.

12th row: P1, m1p, p2, patt to end.

13th row: K2, k2tog, patt to last 4 sts, k3, m1k, k1. [37 (39: 42: 45: 48: 51) sts.]

14th row: P1, m1p, p4, patt to end.

15th row: Patt to last 6 sts, k3, yo, k2tog, m1k, k1.

16th row: P1, m1p, p6, patt to end. [40 (42: 45: 48: 51: 54) sts.]

1st size only: Cont in patt with front edge st in st-st, work 26 rows.

All other sizes: Cont in patt with front edge st in st-st, work 6 rows.

Dec row: (RS) K2, k2tog, patt to end.

Cont in patt, dec in this way at beg of foll 10th row. Patt 9 rows.

All sizes: [40 (40: 43: 46: 49: 52) sts.]

Inc row: (RS) K1, kfb, patt to end.

Cont in patt, inc in this way at beg of 2 (5: 5: 5: 5: 5) foll 6th rows. [43 (46: 49: 52: 55: 58) sts.]

Patt 35 (17: 17: 17: 17: 17) rows.

Shape Armhole and Neck

1st row: (RS) Cast off 3 (4: 4: 5: 6: 6) sts, patt to end.

2nd and every WS row: Patt to end.

3rd row: Skpo, patt to end.

5th row: Skpo, patt to last 2 sts, skpo.

Working sk2po at neck edge when necessary to keep pattern correct, dec one st at each end of next 2 (4: 4: 5: 6: 8) RS rows. [33 (31: 34: 34: 34: 33) sts.]

Cont in patt, dec one st at neck edge on next 6 (4: 4: 3: 2: 0) RS rows. [27 (27: 30: 31: 32: 33) sts.]

Cont in patt, dec one st at neck edge on 8 foll 4th rows. [19 (19: 22: 23: 24: 25) sts.]

Patt 1 row.

Next row: (RS) Patt to last 2 sts, p2tog. [18 (18: 21: 22: 23: 24) sts.]

Patt 1 (3: 7: 9: 13: 17) rows. Cast off.

RIGHT FRONT

Cast on 25 (27: 30: 33: 36: 39) sts.

1st row: (RS) K1, m1k, [yo, p2tog, k7] twice, yo, p2tog, k4 (6: 9: 12: 15: 18).

2nd row: P4 (6: 9: 12: 15: 18), [yo, p2tog, p7] twice, yo, p2tog, p1, m1p, p1.

3rd row: K1, m1k, k2, [yo, p2tog, k3, yo, k2tog, k2] twice, yo, p2tog, k4 (6: 9: 12: 15: 18).

4th row: P4 (6: 9: 12: 15: 18), [yo, p2tog, p7] twice, yo, p2tog, p3, m1p, p1.

5th row: K1, m1k, k4, * yo, p2tog, k2, [yo, k2tog] twice, k1, rep from * once more, yo, p2tog, k4 (6: 9: 12: 15: 18).

6th row: P4 (6: 9: 12: 15: 18), [yo, p2tog, p7] twice, yo, p2tog, p5, m1p, p1. [31 (33: 36: 39: 42: 45) sts.]

These 6 rows set patt to match back with incs at front edge.

7th row: K1, m1k, k6, patt to end.

8th row: Patt to last 8 sts, p7, m1p, p1.

9th row: K1, yo, p1, patt to end.

10th row: Patt to last 3 sts, yo, p2tog, m1p, p1.

11th row: K1, m1k, k1, yo, p2tog, patt to end.

12th row: Patt to last 3 sts, p2, m1p, p1.

13th row: K1, m1k, k3, patt to last 4 sts, skpo, k2. [37 (39: 42: 45: 48: 51) sts.]

14th row: Patt to last 5 sts, p4, m1p, p1.

15th row: K1, m1k, k1, yo, k2tog, k2, patt to end.

16th row: Patt to last 7 sts, p6, m1p, p1. [40 (42: 45: 48: 51: 54) sts.]

1st size only: Cont in patt with front edge st in st-st, work 26 rows.

All other sizes: Cont in patt with front edge st in st-st, work 6 rows.

Dec row: (RS) Patt to last 4 sts, skpo, k2. Cont in patt, dec in this way at end of foll 10th row.

Patt 9 rows.

All sizes: [40 (40: 43: 46: 49: 52) sts.]

Inc row: (RS) Patt to last 3 sts, kfb, k2.

Cont in patt, inc in this way at end of 2 (5: 5: 5: 5: 5) foll 6th rows. [43 (46: 49: 52: 55: 58) sts.]

Patt 35 (17: 17: 17: 17: 17) rows.

Shape Armhole and Neck

1st row: (RS) Patt to end.

2nd row: Cast off 3 (4: 4: 5: 6: 6) sts, patt to end.

3rd row: Patt to last 2 sts, k2tog. Patt 1 row.

5th row: K2tog, patt to last 2 sts, k2tog.

Working k3tog at neck edge when necessary to keep pattern correct, dec one st at each end of next 2 (4: 4: 5: 6: 8) RS rows. [33 (31: 34: 34: 34: 33) sts.]

Cont in patt, dec one st at neck edge on next 6 (4: 4: 3: 2: 0) RS rows. [27 (27: 30: 31: 32: 33) sts.]

Cont in patt, dec one st at neck edge on 8 foll 4th rows. [19 (19: 22: 23: 24: 25) sts.] Patt 1 row.

Next row: (RS) P2tog, patt to end. [18 (18: 21: 22: 23: 24) sts.]

Patt 1 (3: 7: 9: 13: 17) rows. Cast off.

TO MAKE UP

Press according to ball band. Matching sts, join shoulders. Join side seams.

Frill Edging

With RS facing, beg at right side seam, k up 22 (24: 27: 30: 33: 36) sts to start of front shaping, 18 sts around curve, 60 sts up straight edge of right front, 40 (42: 45: 46: 49: 50) sts up right front neck, 36 sts across back neck, 40 (42: 45: 46: 49: 50) sts down left front neck, 60 sts down straight edge of left front, 18 sts around curve, 22 (24: 27: 30: 33: 36) sts to left side seam and 80 (84: 88: 92: 96: 100) sts across lower edge of back. [396 (408: 424: 436: 452: 464) sts.]

[P 1 round, k 1 round] twice. P 1 round. Work in patt.

1st round: [K2, yo, p2tog] to end.

2nd round: [K2, p2tog, yo] to end.

Work last 2 rounds 5 more times.

13th round: [K1, yo, k1, yo, p2tog] to end. [495 (510: 530: 545: 565: 580) sts.]

14th round: [K3, p2tog, yo] to end.

15th round: [K3, yo, p2tog] to end.

16th round: * [K1, yo] 3 times, p2tog, yo, rep from * to end. [792 (816: 848: 872: 904: 928) sts.]

- You'll find it easier to pick up the stitches for the frill edging evenly if you place markers for each section.
- You could fasten your top with a satin ribbon or use leftover yarn to knit a tie. If you prefer, you could wrap the frill edging over and pin with a brooch.

17th round: [K5, p3] to end.

Picot cast-off round: K2, cast off one st, * return st to left needle, cast on 2 sts, cast off 4 sts, rep from * ending last rep cast off 2, fasten off.

Armhole Edgings

With RS facing, k up 88 (92: 96: 100: 104: 108) sts around armhole.

1st round: P.

2nd round: [K2, p2] to end.

3rd round: [K1, yo, k1, p2] to end. [110 (115: 120: 125: 130: 135) sts.]

4th and 5th rounds: [K3, p2] to end.

6th round: [K1, yo, k1, yo, k1, p1, yo, p1] to end. [176 (184: 192: 200: 208: 216) sts.]

7th round: [K5, p3] to end.

Work picot cast-off round as given for frill edging.

Press edgings. Fold frill edging back to form collar. Try on bolero and mark where to fasten it. Sew a small loop of yarn reinforced with buttonhole stitch on pick up row of frill edging at marker on each front. Slip tie through loops to fasten.

This shapely jacket is very quick and easy to knit. It's all in stocking stitch using a feathery yarn that makes a rich, textured fabric, so there's no need for separate bands or edgings.

Crushed Velvet Jacket

EASY

MEASUREMENTS

To fit bust

in.	32	34	36	38	40	42
cm	81	86	91	97	102	107

Actual bust

in.	33½	35½	37½	39½	41¼	43¼
cm	85	90	95	100	105	110

Actual length

in.	21¾	22¼	22½	23	23½	24
cm	55.5	56.5	57.5	58.5	60	61

Actual sleeve length

in.	18
cm	46

In the instructions, figures are given for the smallest size first; larger sizes follow in brackets. Where only one figure is given, this applies to all sizes.

MATERIALS

- 6 (7: 8: 9: 10: 11) × 1¾ oz. (50 g) balls of Sirdar Boa in Damask Rose, 0024
- Pair of size 9 (6 mm) knitting needles
- 4 buttons

TENSION

- 16 sts and 19 rows to 4 in. (10 cm) over st-st on size 9 (6 mm) needles. Change needle size if necessary to obtain this tension.

ABBREVIATIONS

- [ ] – work instructions in square brackets as directed

See also page 12.

NOTES

- The needle size and tension given are larger than usually used for Sirdar Boa. This creates a soft fabric that drapes to enhance the shape of the jacket.
- Mark the RS of the fabric directly after working the first row with a safety pin or loop of contrast thread. The smooth side of st-st is the right side for the garment but it is hard to tell at a glance.
- When working the jacket, use a loop of contrasting smooth thread to mark each shaping. Leave the markers in and use them to match the shapings when sewing up.
- Cast on by the knitting-off-the-thumb method (see pages 14–15).
- Take care to tension the first stitch at the front edges firmly to keep the front edges neat.

○ To check your tension, cast on 20 sts. Use two lengths of contrast color smooth thread as markers. 1st row (RS) K2, take first marker thread between needles to WS of work, k16, take second marker thread to WS of work, k2. 2nd row P2, take marker thread to RS of work, p16, take marker thread to RS of work, p2. Cont in st-st for 17 more rows, weaving marker threads between rows in this way. Cast off. To check your stitch tension, measure between the marker threads. To check your row tension, measure the length of the swatch, omitting cast-on and cast-off edges. If the marked area measures more than 4 in. (10 cm), try again using smaller needles, if it measures less than 4 in. (10 cm), try again using larger needles.

BACK

Cast on 68 (72: 76: 80: 84: 88) sts.

Beg k row, st-st 6 rows.

Dec row: (RS) K1, k2tog, k to last 3 sts, skpo, k1.

Cont in st-st, dec in this way at each end of 3 foll 8th rows. [60 (64: 68: 72: 76: 80) sts.]

St-st 9 rows.

Inc row: (RS) Kfb, k to last 2 sts, kfb, k1.

Cont in st-st, inc in this way at each end of 3 foll 8th rows. [68 (72: 76: 80: 84: 88) sts.]

St-st 5 rows.

Shape Armholes

Cast off 3 sts at beg of next 2 rows.

Dec in same way as before at each end of next 3 (4: 5: 6: 7: 8) RS rows. [56 (58: 60: 62: 64: 66) sts.]

St-st 29 rows. Cast off.

LEFT FRONT

Cast on 37 (39: 41: 43: 45: 47) sts.

Beg k row, st-st 6 rows.

Dec row: (RS) K1, k2tog, k to end.

Cont in st-st, dec in this way at beg of 3 foll 8th rows. [33 (35: 37: 39: 41: 43) sts.]

St-st 9 rows.

Inc row: (RS) Kfb, k to end.

Cont in st-st, inc in this way at beg of 3 foll 8th rows. [37 (39: 41: 43: 45: 47) sts.]

P 1 row.

Shape Neck and Armhole

1st dec row: (RS) K to last 3 sts, skpo, k1.

Cont in st-st, dec in this way at end of next RS row. P 1 row.

Next row: (RS) Cast off 3 sts, k to last 3 sts, skpo, k1. [31 (33: 35: 37: 39: 41) sts.] P 1 row.

2nd dec row: (RS) K1, k2tog, k to last 3 sts, skpo, k1.

Cont in st-st, dec at each end of next 2 (3: 4: 5: 6: 7) RS rows. 25 sts.

Cont in st-st dec as 1st dec row at end of next 12 (11: 10: 10: 9: 8) RS rows. [13 (14: 15: 15: 16: 17) sts.]

St-st 5 (7: 9: 9: 11: 13) rows. Cast off.

Place markers for 4 buttons, the top one just below the neck shaping with 3 more spaced 12 rows apart.

RIGHT FRONT

Cast on 37 (39: 41: 43: 45: 47) sts.

Beg k, st-st 6 rows.

Dec row: (RS) K to last 3 sts, skpo, k1.

Making buttonholes opposite markers, cont in st-st, dec in this way at end of 3 foll 8th rows. [33 (35: 37: 39: 41: 43) sts.]

Buttonhole row: (RS) K3, yo, k2tog, k to end.

St-st 9 rows.

Inc row: (RS) K to last 2 sts, kfb, k1.

Cont in st-st, inc in this way at end of 3 foll 8th rows. [37 (39: 41: 43: 45: 47) sts.]

P 1 row.

- It's easier to count the rows on the wrong side by running your thumbnail down the rows and counting the bumps.
- To check the length by measuring rather than counting rows, the jacket should measure approximately 14½ in. (36.5 cm) to the armholes and 21¾ (22¼: 22½: 23: 24) in., 55.5 (56.5: 57.5: 58.5: 60: 61) cm to the shoulders. Make sure that you spread the garment out to its full width before measuring or you could find that your measurements are not accurate.

Shape Neck and Armhole

1st dec row: K1, k2tog, k to end.

Cont in st-st, dec in this way at beg of next 2 RS rows.

Next row: (WS) Cast off 3 sts, p to end. [31 (33: 35: 37: 39: 41) sts.]

2nd dec row: (RS) K1, k2tog, k to last 3 sts, skpo, k1.

Cont in st-st, dec at each end of next 2 (3: 4: 5: 6: 7) RS rows. [25 sts.]

Cont in st-st dec as 1st dec row at beg of next 12 (11: 10: 10: 9: 8) RS rows. [13 (14: 15: 15: 16: 17) sts.] St-st 5 (7: 9: 9: 11: 13) rows. Cast off.

SLEEVES

Cast on 33 (33: 35: 35: 37: 37) sts.

Beg k, st-st 8 (6: 6: 4: 8: 8) rows.

Inc row: (RS) Kfb, k to last 2 sts, kfb, k1.

Cont in st-st, inc in this way at each end of 8 (9: 9: 10: 10: 11) foll 8th (8th: 8th: 8th: 6th: 6th) rows. [51 (53: 55: 57: 59: 61) sts.]

St-st 15 (9: 9: 3: 19: 13) rows.

Shape Top

Cast off 3 sts at beg of next 2 rows.

Dec in same way as before at each end of next 11 (12: 13: 14: 15: 16) RS rows. [23 sts.]

P 1 row.

Cast off.

TO MAKE UP

Matching sts, join shoulders. Set in sleeves. Join side and sleeve seams. Sew on buttons.

Turn heads when you turn around in this sophisticated slimline sweater.

V-Back Sweater

MEASUREMENTS

To fit bust

in.	32	34	36	38	40	42
cm	81	86	91	97	102	107

Actual measurement across front

in.	16	17¼	18½	19¾	20½	21½
cm	41	44	47	50	52	55

Actual length

in.	20	20½	20¾	21¼	21¼	22
cm	51	52	53	54	54	56

Actual sleeve length

in.	12½
cm	32

In the instructions, figures are given for the smallest size first; larger sizes follow in brackets. Where only one figure is given, this applies to all sizes.

MATERIALS

- 7 (7: 8: 8: 8: 9) x 1¾ oz. (50 g) balls of Debbie Bliss Cathay in purple, 12
- Pair each of size 2 or 3 (3 mm) and size 5 (3.75 mm) knitting needles
- Size 5 (3.75 mm) circular needle, 39½ in. (100 cm) long

TENSION

- 22 sts and 30 rows to 4 in. (10 cm) over st-st on size 5 (3.75 mm) needles.

ABBREVIATIONS

See page 12.

FRONT

Using size 2 or 3 (3 mm) needles, cast on 88 (94: 100: 106: 112: 118) sts.

1st rib row: (RS) P1, * k2, p1; rep from * to end.

2nd rib row: K1, * p2, k1; rep from * to end.

Rep these 2 rows 6 times more. Change to size 5 (3.75 mm) needles. Beg k row, st-st 4 rows.

1st dec row: (RS) K1, skpo, k to last 3 sts, k2tog, k1. **

Cont to dec in this way at each end of every foll 6th row 4 times. [78 (84: 90: 96: 102: 108) sts.]

Beg and ending p row, st-st 7 rows straight.

1st inc row: (RS) K2, m1, k to last 2 sts, m1, k2.

Cont to inc in this way at each end of every foll 8th row 6 times. [92 (98: 104: 110: 116: 122) sts.]

Beg and ending p row, st-st 5 rows straight.

○ Instead of slipping "waiting" stitches on to a spare needle, leave them on a length of contrast yarn for lightness and flexibility.

Shape Armholes

Cast off 3 (3: 3: 4: 4: 4) sts at beg of next 2 rows.

Next row: (RS) K1, skpo, k to last 3 sts, k2tog, k1.

Cont to dec in this way at each end of next 8 (9: 10: 10: 11: 12) RS rows. [68 (72: 76: 80: 84: 88) sts.]

Beg and ending p row, st-st 17 (17: 19: 19: 19: 21) rows straight.

Neck Shaping

1st row: (RS) K21 (23: 25: 27: 28: 30) sts, turn.

Cont on these sts only for first side and leave rem sts on a spare needle.

2nd row: P3, k1, p to end.

3rd row: K to last 6 sts, skpo, p1, k3.

Rep last 2 rows twice more. [18 (20: 22: 24: 25: 27) sts.]

Patt 10 (10: 10: 12: 12: 12) rows straight – patt means working one stitch rib 3 sts in from neck edge.

Cast off.

Next row: (RS) Slip center 26 (26: 26: 26: 28: 28) sts on to a spare needle, k to end.

Next row: P to last 4 sts, k1, p3.

Next row: K3, p1, k2tog, k to end.

Complete to match first side.

BACK

Using size 2 or 3 (3 mm) needles, cast on 82 (88: 94: 100: 106: 112) sts.

Work as front to **. Cont to dec in this way at each end of every foll 6th row 4 times more, so ending with with a RS row. [72 (78: 84: 90: 96: 102) sts.]

Next row: P32 (35: 38: 41: 44: 47), k1, p6, k1, p32 (35: 38: 41: 44: 47).

Shape Center and Side

1st row: (RS) K30 (33: 36: 39: 42: 45), skpo, p1, k3, turn.

Cont on these sts only for first side and leave rem sts on a spare needle.

2nd and WS rows: P3, k1, p to end.

3rd row: K to last 6 sts, skpo, p1, k3.

5th row: As 3rd row.

7th row: K2, m1, k to last 4 sts, p1, k3.

Cont to inc in this way at side edge on every foll 8th row 6 times more while at the same time dec as before at center edge on next RS row and every foll 4th row until a total of 7 (7: 8: 8: 9: 9) dec rows has been completed at center edge, then dec at center edge on every foll 6th row 6 (6: 5: 5: 5: 5) times. [30 (33: 36: 39: 41: 44) sts.]

Patt 3 (3: 5: 5: 1: 1) rows straight, so ending with a WS row.

Shape Armhole

Cast off 3 (3: 3: 4: 4: 4) sts at beg of next row.

Next RS row: K1, skpo, k to last 4 sts, p1, k3.

Cont to dec in this way at beg of next 8 (9: 10: 10: 11: 12) RS rows. [18 (20: 22: 24: 25: 27) sts.]

Patt straight until work matches front to shoulder, so ending with a WS row. Cast off.

Next row: (RS) Rejoin yarn to inner end of rem sts, k3, p1, k2tog, k to end.

Complete to match first side, working one more row to armhole and working decs as k2tog.

SLEEVES

With size 2 or 3 (3 mm) needles, cast on 46 (49: 52: 52: 55: 58) sts.

Rib 14 rows as front. Change to size 5 (3.75 mm) needles. Beg k row, st-st 6 (6: 6: 4: 4: 4) rows straight.

Next row: (RS) K2, m1, k to last 2 sts, m1, k2.

Cont to inc in this way at each end of every foll 10th (10th: 10th: 8th: 8th: 8th) row 7 (7: 7: 9: 9: 9) times. [62 (65: 68: 72: 75: 78) sts.]

Cont straight until work measures 12½ in. (32 cm), ending p row.

Shape Top

Cast off 3 (3: 3: 4: 4: 4) sts at beg of next 2 rows.

Next row: (RS) K1, skpo, k to last 3 sts, k2tog, k1.

Cont to dec in this way at each end of next 8 (9: 10: 10: 11: 12) RS rows. [38 (39: 40: 42: 43: 44) sts.]

Dec as before at each end of every foll 4th row 4 times. [30 (31: 32: 34: 35: 36) sts.]

Cast off 2 sts at beg of next 6 rows. Cast off rem 18 (19: 20: 22: 23: 24) sts purlwise.

NECK EDGING

Join right shoulder seam.

With RS facing and using size 5 (3.75 mm) circular needle, pick up and k14 (14: 14: 16: 16: 16) sts down left front neck, k26 (26: 26: 26: 28: 28) sts from front neck, pick up and k14 (14: 14: 16: 16: 16) sts up right front neck, 86 (88: 90: 92: 92: 96) sts down right back and 86 (88: 90: 92: 92: 96) sts up left back. [226 (230: 234: 242: 244: 252) sts.]

Turn and cast off knitwise, working skpo in last 2 sts before center V at back and k2tog in first 2 sts after center V.

TO MAKE UP

Join left shoulder seam. Press according to ball band. Set in sleeves. Join side and sleeve seams.

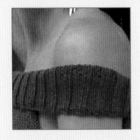

Show off your shoulders and look like a film star when you wear this slinky top.

Off-the-Shoulder Top

MEASUREMENTS

To fit bust

in.	32	34	36	38	40	42
cm	81	86	91	97	102	107

Actual bust

in.	32¼	33¾	35¾	38	40	41¾
cm	82	86	91	97	102	106

Actual length to underarm

in.	15¾	15¾	15¾	15¾	15¾	15¾
cm	40	40	40	40	40	40

In the instructions, figures are given for the smallest size first; larger sizes follow in brackets. Where only one figure is given, this applies to all sizes.

MATERIALS

- 6 (7: 7: 7: 8: 8) x 1¾ oz. (50 g) balls Debbie Bliss Cashmerino Aran in blue, 208
- Pair each of size 6 (4 mm) and size 8 (5 mm) knitting needles
- Size 6 (4 mm) circular needle, 31½ in. (80 cm) long

TENSION

- 18 sts and 24 rows to 4 in. (10 cm) over st-st on size 8 (5 mm) needles.

ABBREVIATIONS

- [ ] – work instructions in square brackets as directed

See also page 12.

FRONT

Using size 6 (4 mm) needles, cast on 90 (94: 98: 106: 110: 114) sts.

1st rib row: (RS) K2, * p2, k2; rep from * to end.

2nd rib row: P2, * k2, p2; rep from * to end.

Rep these 2 rows 8 times more, then work 1st rib row again.

Next row: (WS) Rib 2 (2: 2: 6: 6: 6), [k2tog, rib 6] 5 times, k2tog, rib 2 (6: 10: 10: 14: 18), [k2tog, rib 6] 5 times, k2tog, rib 2 (2: 2: 6: 6: 6). [78 (82: 86: 94: 98: 102) sts.]

Change to size 8 (5 mm) needles. Beg k row, st-st 4 rows.

1st dec row: (RS) K21 (22: 23: 25: 26: 27), k2tog, k32 (34: 36: 40: 42: 44), skpo, k 21 (22: 23: 25: 26: 27). Beg p row, st-st 3 rows.

○ Cable cast-on for cuff: * k in first st on left-hand needle but do not slip it off, put the new loop from the right needle on to the left needle; rep from *, inserting right needle between first and 2nd sts to make each new st.

2nd dec row: (RS) K21 (22: 23: 25: 26: 27), k2tog, k30 (32: 34: 38: 40: 42), skpo, k21 (22: 23: 25: 26: 27).

Cont to dec in this way, working 2 sts less between each pair of decs, on every foll 4th row until a total of 7 dec rows has been completed. [64 (68: 72: 80: 84: 88) sts.]

Beg and ending p row, st-st 7 (7: 7: 9: 9: 9) rows straight.

1st inc row: (RS) K21 (22: 23: 25: 26: 27), m1, k to last 21 (22: 23: 25: 26: 27) sts, m1, k 21 (22: 23: 25: 26: 27).

Cont to inc in this way on every foll 8th (8th: 8th: 10th: 10th: 10th) row 4 (4: 4: 3: 3: 3) times. [74 (78: 82: 88: 92: 96) sts.]

Beg and ending p row, st-st 11 rows straight.

Shape Armholes

Cast off 6 (6: 6: 7: 7: 7) sts at beg of next 2 rows.

Next row: (RS) K2, k2tog, k to last 4 sts, skpo, k2. **

Cont to dec in this way on next 6 (7: 8: 9: 10: 11) RS rows, so ending with a RS row. [48 (50: 52: 54: 56: 58) sts.] Leave sts on a spare needle.

BACK

As front to **.

Cont to dec in this way on next 2 (3: 4: 5: 6: 7) RS rows. [56 (58: 60: 62: 64: 66) sts.]

St-st 14 rows straight, so ending with a RS row.

Do not break yarn.

CUFF

Sl sts of back on to size 6 (4 mm) circular needle, using attached yarn and with WS facing, cast on by cable method (see note left) 26 (30: 34: 38: 42: 44) sts, turn and with RS facing, k48 (50: 52: 54: 56: 58) sts of front, turn, cast on 26 (30: 34: 38: 42: 44) sts, turn, k56 (58: 60: 62: 64: 66) sts of back. [156 (168: 180: 192: 204: 212) sts.]

With RS facing, work in rounds.

1st round: * K2, p2; rep from * to end.

Rep this round 12 times more.

14th round: * Kfb, k1, p2; rep from * to end.

15th round: * K3, p2; rep from * to end.

Rep last round 14 times more.

Cast off loosely in rib.

ARMHOLE EDGING

Join side seams.

With RS facing and using size 6 (4 mm) circular needle, pick up and k22 (24: 26: 28: 32) sts around left back armhole, one st from side seam and 18 (20: 22: 24: 28) sts around left front armhole. [41 (45: 49: 53: 61) sts.]

Cast off knitwise.

Work right armhole to match.

TO MAKE UP

Press st-st according to instructions on ball band. Catch down ends of armhole edging. Turn cuff in half to RS.

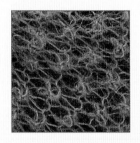

This flattering, wispy little top won't keep you warm but will add oodles of glamour to any outfit.

Lightweight Shrug

ADVANCED

MEASUREMENTS

Stretches to fit bust

in.	32	34	36	38
cm	81	86	91	97

Actual bust

in.	30½	33¼	35½	38¼
cm	77.5	84.5	90.5	97.5

Actual length

in.	13	13½	15	15½
cm	33	34	38	39

Actual sleeve length

in.	10
cm	25

In the instructions, figures are given for the smallest size first; larger sizes follow in brackets. Where only one figure is given, this applies to all sizes.

MATERIALS

- 3 (3: 4: 4) × 1 oz. (25 g) balls of Rowan Kid Silk Haze in Jelly, 597
- Pair of size 7 (4.5 mm) knitting needles
- E4 (3.5 mm) crochet hook

TENSION

- 24 sts and 24 rows to 4 in. (10 cm) over blackberry stitch on size 7 (4.5 mm) needles. Change needle size if necessary to obtain this tension.

ABBREVIATIONS

- **dc** – double crochet
- **[ ]** – work instructions in square brackets as directed

See also page 12.

NOTE

- To cast on at the end of a row, loop yarn around left thumb and slip loop on to right needle for each stitch.

- The needle size is bigger than usually used for Rowan Kid Silk Haze to add to the lacy effect.
- You may find it easier to knit with the weight of the right needle supported under the right arm.
- The fronts start with the tie and are worked sideways, ending at the side seam.
- When shaping the fronts, the increases are integrated with the pattern so when a yarn over increase is made on the right side row, an increase group is worked into it on the next row.

BACK

Cast on 95 (99: 103: 107) sts.

1st and 3rd rows: (RS) P.

2nd row: P1, * [k1, p1, k1] in next st, p3tog, rep from * to last 2 sts, [k1, p1, k1] in next st, p1. [97 (101: 105: 109) sts.]

4th row: P1, * p3tog, [k1, p1, k1] in next st, rep from * to last 4 sts, p3tog, p1. [95 (99: 103: 107) sts.] These 4 rows form blackberry st patt.

Work 28 (28: 32: 32) more rows, so ending with a 4th patt row.

Shape Armholes

1st row: (RS) Cast off 5 (5: 9: 9) sts purlwise, p to end.

2nd row: Cast off 5 (5: 9: 9) sts knitwise, one st on right needle, beg p3tog, patt as 4th row to end. [83 (87: 83: 87) sts.]

3rd row: P2tog, p to last 2 sts, p2tog. [81 (85: 81: 85) sts.]

4th row: Work as given for 4th patt row. [79 (83: 79: 83) sts.]

Work 3rd and 4th rows 2 (2: 0: 0) more times. [71 (75: 79: 83) sts.]

Patt 40 (42: 52: 54) rows straight. [71 (77: 79: 85) sts.] Cast off.

RIGHT FRONT

Cast on 3 sts.

1st row: (RS) P.

2nd row: P1, [k1, p1, k1] in next st, p1. [5 sts.]

3rd, 5th, 7th, and 9th rows: P1, yo, p to last st, yo, p1.

4th row: P1, [k1, p1, k1] in next st, p3tog, [k1, p1, k1] in next st, p1. [9 sts.]

6th row: P1, * [k1, p1, k1] in next st, p3tog, rep from * once, [k1, p1, k1] in next st, p1. [13 sts.]

8th row: P1, * [k1, p1, k1] in next st, p3tog, rep from * twice, [k1, p1, k1] in next st, p1, [17 sts.]

10th row: P1, * [k1, p1, k1] in next st, p3tog, rep from * 3 times, [k1, p1, k1] in next st, p1. [21 sts.]

11th and 13th rows: P.

12th row: P1, * p3tog, [k1, p1, k1] in next st, rep from * 3 times, p3tog, p1. [19 sts.]

14th row: P1, * [k1, p1, k1] in next st, p3tog, rep from * 3 times, [k1, p1, k1] in next st, p1. [21 sts.]

Work 11th to 14th rows 4 more times. [21 sts.]

Shape Front

1st inc row: (RS) P1, yo, p to last st, yo, p1. [23 sts.]

2nd inc row: P1, * [k1, p1, k1] in next st, p3tog, rep from * to last 2 sts, [k1, p1, k1] in next st, p1. [25 sts.]

Work 1st and 2nd inc rows 4 more times. [41 sts **.]

Shape Neck

Next row: P1, yo, p to end. 42 sts.

Next row: P1, * p3tog, [k1, p1, k1] in next st, rep from * to last st, p1. [42 sts.]

Keeping patt at lower edge straight, inc by working p1, yo at neck edge on next 4 (5: 6: 7) RS rows. [50 (51: 54: 55) sts.]

Patt 1 row. [50 (53: 54: 57) sts.] Do not turn.

○ The blackberry stitch pattern is worked by alternately making three stitches from one and taking three stitches together. Where there is an increase group at each end of a row, the stitch count increases by two, where there is a decrease group at each end of a row, the stitch count decreases by two. Where there is an increase group at one end and a decrease group at the other end of a row, the stitch count remains constant. Stitch counts for each change are given throughout.

Shape Shoulder

Cast on 28 (29: 28: 29) sts. [78 (82: 82: 86) sts.]
Noting that st count is constant, beg p row, patt 14 (18: 22: 26) rows, so ending with a WS row.

Shape Armhole

Next row: (RS) Cast off 37 (40: 42: 44) sts purlwise, p to end. [41 (42: 40: 42) sts.]
Next row: Patt, ending, p3tog, p1. [40 (42: 38: 42) sts.]
Keeping patt at lower edge straight, dec by working p2tog at beg of next 4 (4: 2: 2) RS rows and ending WS rows p3tog, p1. [33 (34: 36: 38) sts.]
Noting that st count for 1st and 3rd sizes varies by 2 sts, patt 3 (3: 7: 7) rows. Cast off.

LEFT FRONT

Work as given for right front to **.

Shape Neck

Next row: P to last st, yo, p1. 42 sts.
Next row: P1, * [k1, p1, k1] in next st, p3tog, rep from * to last st, p1. [42 sts.]
Keeping patt at lower edge straight, inc by ending next 4 (5: 6: 7) RS rows yo, pl. [50 (51: 54: 55) sts.]
Patt 1 row. [50 (53: 54: 57) sts.]

Shape Shoulder

Next row: P to end, do not turn, cast on 28 (29: 28: 29) sts. [78 (82: 82: 86) sts.]
Noting that st count is constant, patt 14 (18: 22: 26) rows, so ending with a p row.

Shape Armhole

Next row: (WS) Cast off 37 (40: 41: 44) sts, one st on right needle, beg p3tog, patt to end. [39 (42: 39: 42) sts.]

Keeping patt at lower edge straight, dec by working p2tog at end of next 4 (4: 2: 2) RS rows and beg WS rows pl, p3tog. [33 (34: 37: 38) sts.]

Noting that st count for 1st and 3rd sizes varies by 2 sts, patt 3 (3: 7: 7) rows. Cast off.

SLEEVES

Cast on 99 (99: 111: 111) sts.

Patt 8 rows as given for back, so ending with a 4th patt row.

1st dec row: (RS) P2tog, p to last 2 sts, p2tog.

2nd dec row: Work as given for 4th patt row.

Alternating st count between 97 (97: 109: 109) and 95 (95: 107: 107) sts, patt 8 rows.

Work 1st and 2nd dec rows again.

Alternating st count between 93 (93: 105: 105) and 91 (91: 103: 103) sts, patt 8 rows.

Work 1st and 2nd dec rows again.

Alternating st count between 89 (89: 101: 101) and 87 (87: 99: 99) sts, patt 8 rows.

Work 1st and 2nd dec rows again.

Alternating st count between 85 (85: 97: 97) and 83 (83: 95: 95) sts, patt 20 rows. [83 (83: 95: 95) sts.]

Shape Top

1st row: (RS) Cast off 5 (5: 9: 9) sts purlwise, p to end.

2nd row: Cast off 5 (5: 9: 9) sts knitwise, one st on right needle, beg p3tog, patt to end. [71 (71: 75: 75) sts.]

3rd row: P2tog, p to last 2 sts, p2tog.

4th row: Work as 4th patt row.

Work 3rd and 4th rows 10 more times. [27 (27: 31: 31) sts.]

Cast off 4 sts at beg of next 4 rows. [11 (11: 15: 15) sts.] Cast off.

TO MAKE UP

Matching sts, join shoulders. Set in sleeves. Join side and sleeve seams.

Edging

Using crochet hook and with RS facing, join yarn at right front side seam, skipping sts or row-ends where necessary to keep edge neat, work 63 (67: 71: 75) dc along lower edge to center of tie, 71 (75: 79: 83) dc along tie and up right front neck, 35 (35: 37: 37) dc across back neck, 71 (75: 79: 83) dc down left front neck to center of tie, 63 (67: 71: 75) dc along tie and lower edge of left front and 77 (81: 85: 89) dc across back, join in 1st dc with a slip st, turn. [380 (400: 422: 442) dc.]

Work 1dc in each dc around edge, slip st in 1st dc, fasten off.

Cuff Edgings

Working into each st to flare the edge, join yarn at seam and work to match edging.

Feel nostalgic in this shapely little camisole top with a front cable panel that suggests laced-up ribbon.

Cabled Camisole

INTERMEDIATE

MEASUREMENTS

To fit bust

in.	32	34	36	38	40	42
cm	81	86	91	97	102	107

Actual bust

in.	30¾	32¾	35	37½	39½	41¼
cm	78	83	89	95	100	105

Actual length to underarm

in.	11¾	11¾	12	12	12¼	12¼
cm	30	30	30.5	30.5	31	31

In the instructions, figures are given for the smallest size first; larger sizes follow in brackets. Where only one figure is given, this applies to all sizes.

MATERIALS

- 4 (4: 5: 5: 6: 6) × 1¾ oz. (50 g) balls of Debbie Bliss Cathay in duck egg, 08
- Pair each of size 3 (3.25 mm) and size 5 (3.75 mm) knitting needles
- Cable needle

TENSION

- 22 sts and 30 rows to 4 in. (10 cm) over st-st on size 5 (3.75 mm) needles.

ABBREVIATIONS

- **c3b** – sl one st on to cable needle and hold at back, k2 then k1 from cable needle
- **c3f** – sl 2 sts on to cable needle and hold at front, k1 then k2 from cable needle
- **tbl** – through back of loops

See also page 12.

NOTE

- The panels of cable used in this design are explained both as charts and as row-by-row instructions so that you can choose your preferred method of following the stitch pattern.

Panel A

Worked over 12 sts.

1st row: (RS) P1, k2, c3b, c3f, k2, p1.

2nd and WS rows: P.

3rd row: P1, k1, c3b, k2, c3f, k1, p1.

5th row: P1, c3b, k4, c3f, p1.

7th row: P1, c3f, k4, c3b, p1.

9th row: P1, k1, c3f, k2, c3b, k1, p1.

11th row: P 1, k2, c3f, c3b, k2, p1.

12th row: P.

Panel B

Worked over 24 sts.

1st row: (RS) P1, k2, c3b, k3, c3b, c3f, k3, c3f, k2, p1.

2nd and WS rows: P.

3rd row: P1, k1, c3b, k3, c3b, k2, c3f, k3, c3f, k1, p1.

5th row: P1, c3b, k3, c3b, k4, c3f, k3, c3f, p1.

7th row: P1, k5, c3b, k3, c3b, c3f, k5, p1.

9th row: P1, k4, c3b, k3, c3b, k2, c3f, k4, p1.

11th row: P1, k3, c3b, k3, c3b, k4, c3f, k3, p1.

12th row: P.

BACK

Using size 3 (3.25 mm) needles, cast on 78 (84: 90: 96: 102: 108) sts.

Beg k row, st-st 4 rows. Change to size 5 (3.75 mm) needles and patt:

1st row: (RS) K15 (18: 20: 23: 25: 28), patt 12 sts of 1st row of chart A or 1st row of panel A, k24 (24: 26: 26: 28: 28), patt 12 sts of 1st row of chart A or 1st row of panel A, k15 (18: 20: 23: 25: 28).

2nd and WS rows: P.

3rd row: K15 (18: 20: 23: 25: 28), patt 12 sts of 3rd row of chart A or 3rd row of panel A, k24 (24: 26: 26: 28: 28), patt 12 sts of 3rd row of chart A or 3rd row of panel A, k15 (18: 20: 23: 25: 28).

5th row: K2, skpo, k11 (14: 16: 19: 21: 24), patt 12 sts of 5th row of chart A or 5th row of panel A, k24 (24: 26: 26: 28: 28), patt 12 sts of 5th row of chart A or 5th row of panel A, k11 (14: 16: 19: 21: 24), k2tog, k2.

7th row: K14 (17: 19: 22: 24: 27), patt 12 sts of 7th row of chart A or 7th row of panel A, k24 (24: 26: 26: 28: 28), patt 12 sts of 7th row of chart A or 7th row of panel A, k14 (17: 19: 22: 24: 27).

9th row: K2, skpo, k10 (13: 15: 18: 20: 23), patt 12 sts of 9th row of chart A or 9th row of panel A, k24 (24: 26: 26: 28: 28), patt 12 sts of 9th row of chart A or 9th row of panel A, k10 (13: 15: 18: 20: 23), k2tog, k2.

11th row: K13 (16: 18: 21: 23: 26), patt 12 sts of 11th row of chart A or 11th row of panel A, k24 (24: 26: 26: 28: 28), patt 12 sts of 11th row of chart A or 11th row of panel A, k13 (16: 18: 21: 23: 26).

12th row: P.

These 12 rows form patt. Rep 1st–12th rows while at the same time dec as before at each end of next row and every foll 4th row, working one st less after first dec and one st less before 2nd dec each time, until 6 dec rows have been completed. [66 (72: 78: 84: 90: 96) sts.]

Patt 19 rows straight, so ending with a WS row.

45th row: K3, m1, patt to last 3 sts, m1, k3.

Cont to inc in this way at each end of every foll 6th row until 4 inc rows have been completed. [74 (80: 86: 92: 98: 104) sts.]

Cont to inc at each end of every foll 4th row until a total of 10 inc rows has been completed. [86 (92: 98: 104: 110: 116) sts.]

Patt 3 (3: 5: 5: 7: 7) rows straight, so ending with a WS row.

Shape Armholes and Neck

** Keeping patt correct, cast off 6 (7: 7: 8: 8: 9) sts at beg of next 2 rows.

Next row: (RS) K2, skpo, patt to last 4 sts, k2tog, k2.

Cont to dec in this way on next 4 (4: 6: 6: 8: 8) RS rows. *** [64 (68: 70: 74: 76: 80) sts.]
P one row.

Next row: (RS) K8 (10: 10: 12: 12: 14) sts, turn.
Cont on these sts only for first side and leave rem sts on a spare needle.

Next row: P2tog tbl, p to end.

Next row: K to last 2 sts, skpo.
Rep last 2 rows 2 (3: 3: 4: 4: 5) times more. P2tog tbl. Fasten off.

Next row: (RS) Rejoin yarn to inner end of rem sts; working p1, k1, skpo, k4, k2tog, k1, p1, k24 (24: 26: 26: 28: 28), p1, k1, skpo, k4, k2tog, k1, p1, cast off center 48 (48: 50: 50: 52: 52) sts; k rem 8 (10: 10: 12: 12: 14) sts.

Next row: P to last 2 sts, p2tog.

Next row: K2tog, k to end.
Rep last 2 rows 2 (3: 3: 4: 4: 5) times more. P2tog.
Fasten off.

FRONT

Using size 3 (3.25 mm) needles, cast on 82 (88: 94: 100: 106: 112) sts.
Beg k row, st-st 4 rows. Change to size 5 (3.75 mm) needles and patt:

1st row: (RS) K15 (18: 20: 23: 25: 28), patt 12 sts of 1st row of chart A or panel A, k2 (2: 3: 3: 4: 4), patt 24 sts of 1st row of chart B or panel B, k2 (2: 3: 3: 4: 4), patt 12 sts of 1st row of chart A or panel A, k15 (18: 20: 23: 25: 28).

2nd and WS rows: P.

3rd row: K15 (18: 20: 23: 25: 28), patt 12 sts of 3rd row of chart A or panel A, k2 (2: 3: 3: 4: 4), patt 24 sts of 3rd row of chart B or panel B, k2 (2: 3: 3: 4: 4), patt 12 sts of 3rd row of chart A or panel A, k 15 (18: 20: 23: 25: 28).
Cont to patt as set, dec one st as for back at each end of next RS row and every foll 4th row until 6 dec rows have been completed. [70 (76: 82: 88: 94: 100) sts.]

Chart A

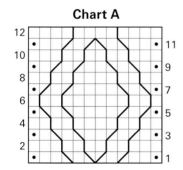

Key

☐ K on RS rows, p on WS rows

⊡ P on RS rows

◿◺ Sl 1 st on to cable needle and hold at back, k2 then k1 from cable needle (c3b)

◣◢ Sl 2 sts on to cable needle and hold at front, k1 then k2 from cable needle (c3f)

Note: Read all odd-numbered RS rows from right to left.

Chart B

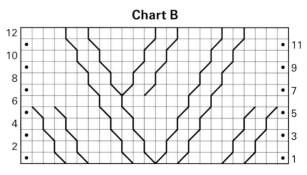

Patt 19 rows straight, so ending with a WS row.

Inc as for back at each end of next and every foll 6th row until 4 inc rows has been completed. [78 (84: 90: 96: 102: 108) sts.]

Cont to inc at each end of every foll 4th row until a total of 10 inc rows have been completed. [90 (96: 102: 108: 114: 120) sts.]

Patt 3 (3: 5: 5: 7: 7) rows straight, so ending with a WS row.

Shape Armholes and Neck

As back from ** to ***. [68 (72: 74: 78: 80: 84) sts.] P one row.

Next row: (RS) K8 (10: 10: 12: 12: 14) sts, turn.

Cont on these sts only for first side and leave rem sts on a spare needle.

Next row: P2tog tbl, p to end.

Next row: K to last 2 sts, skpo.

Rep last 2 rows 2 (3: 3: 4: 4: 5) times more. P2tog tbl. Fasten off.

Next row: (RS) Rejoin yarn to inner end of rem sts; working p1, k1, skpo, k4, k2tog, k1, p1, k2 (2: 3: 3: 4: 4), p1, k1, skpo, k4, skpo, k4, k2tog, k4, k2tog, k1, p1, k2 (2: 3: 3: 4: 4), p1, k1, skpo, k4, k2tog, k1, p1, cast off center 52 (52: 54: 54: 56: 56) sts, k rem 8 (10: 10: 12: 12: 14) sts.

Complete as 2nd side of back.

BAND

Join side seams, reversing seams for first 4 rows at cast-on edge.

Using size 3 (3.25 mm) needles, cast on 6 sts.

1st row: (RS) P1, k4, p1.

2nd row: P.

3rd row: P1, sl next 2 sts on to cable needle and hold at back, k2 then k2 from cable needle, p1.

4th row: P.

These 4 rows form patt. Rep 1st–4th rows until band, slightly stretched, fits around back neck, over shoulder, around front neck and over shoulder. Cast off.

ARMHOLE EDGING

With RS facing and using size 5 (3.75 mm) needles, pick up and k21 (23: 26: 28: 31: 33) sts around left back armhole and 21 (23: 26: 28: 31: 33) sts around left front armhole. 42 (46: 52: 56: 62: 66) sts.

Cast off knitwise.

Work right armhole to match.

TO MAKE UP

Press lightly according to ball band. Join ends of band and, seam to the back, sew to back and front neck.

Carry all of your party essentials in this easy-to-make beaded clutch bag.

Beaded Clutch Bag

EASY

MEASUREMENTS

Actual width
in.   9½
cm   24

Actual height
in.   5½
cm   14

MATERIALS

o 2 × 1¾ oz. (50 g) hanks of Debbie Bliss
  Pure Silk in turquoise, 07
o Pair of size 3 (3.25 mm) knitting needles
o 2,256 medium glass/seed beads (size 5/0)
o Heavy, iron-on interlining – one piece 9½
  × 10½ in. (24 × 27 cm) and one piece 9½ ×
  17 in. (24 × 43 cm)
o Lining fabric – one piece 10½ × 18 in. (27
  × 46 cm) and two pieces 3¼ × 5 in. (8.5 ×
  13 cm)
o Matching sewing thread and a sharp
  needle
o Press stud or magnetic bag catch
  (optional)
o Round pierced metal brooch form and
  assorted beads (optional)

TENSION

o 21 sts and 30 rows to 4 in. (10 cm) over
  beaded reverse st-st, 25 sts and 35 rows to
  4 in. (10 cm) over st-st on size 3 (3.25 mm)
  needles. Change needle size if necessary
  to obtain these tensions.

ABBREVIATIONS

o **B** – bring a bead up close to the work
o [ ] – work instructions in square brackets
  as directed
See also page 12.

NOTES

o This kind of knitting is easy to do because
  the beads lie between the stitches.
o The bag is knitted using smaller needles
  than usual for Debbie Bliss Pure Silk to
  give a firm fabric.
o You only need to thread beads onto the
  yarn for the bag flap, the rest of the bag is
  knitted without beads.
o Check the size of your bag before cutting
  the lining and interlining. If your tension
  is not correct, your bag will be a different
  size and you will need to adjust the
  measurements.

- The medium-size seed beads used for the bag are often called size 5 or 5/0. They are colored glass with a shiny, silvery lining.
- You can use any beads for your bag—pearly, metallic, or clear glass. You could even work in stripes of different colors. Just make sure that you choose beads with a hole that's big enough to thread them on to the yarn.
- It is probably only practical to thread between 300 and 500 beads on to the yarn at a time. When you don't have enough beads left to work a row, cut the yarn at the beginning of a row, add more beads and rejoin the yarn. Never join in new yarn during a row.
- The type of heavyweight iron-on interlining that you need is often labelled as suitable for collar stiffening or for tie-backs, pelmets, and furnishings.
- If you can't find a heavyweight iron-on interlining, you could use a non-iron interlining and hold it in place with stitching.
- A size 10 quilting needle makes small neat stitches when sewing the lining, but you could use any type of sharp needle or if you prefer, a sewing machine.

FLAP

Using beaded yarn, cast on 51 sts.
K 1 row.
1st row: (RS) P2, [B, p1] to last st, p1.
2nd row: K2, [B, k1] to last st, k1.
These 2 rows form beaded reverse st-st.
Work 45 more rows. Cast off loosely.

BACK AND FRONT

Using yarn without beads, cast on 60 sts.
Beg k row, st-st 97 rows. Cast off knitwise.

SIDE PANELS

(Make 2) Using yarn without beads, cast on 14 sts. Beg k row, st-st 35 rows. Cast off knitwise.

TO MAKE UP

Join cast-off edge of flap to cast-off edge of back and front. Leaving one stitch free at each side and 2 rows free at cast-on edge, fuse the 9½ x 10½ in. (24 x 27 cm) piece of interlining to the back and front of bag. Using mattress stitch and taking one stitch into seam, leaving 2 rows at cast-on edge of back and front of bag free, set in side panels. Leaving ½ in. (1.5 cm) of lining free all around, fuse the 9½ x 17 in. (24 x 43 cm), piece of iron-on interlining to the 10½ x 18 in. (27 x 46 cm) piece of lining fabric. With raw edge of seam allowance on same side as interlining and leaving approximately 6¼ in. (16 cm) free at one end for flap lining, set in lining side pieces. Press in all seam allowances.

Placing interlinings together, insert lining into bag. If using a magnetic bag catch or other catch it may be necessary to insert it at this stage. Fix according to manufacturer's instructions. Slip stitch lining in place. Catch tops of side panels together.

If not using a bag catch, sew press stud on front and flap of bag.

For the optional decoration, stitch beads to the pierced metal form and sew on bag.

Shimmer and Shine

Go for full-on nighttime glamour or glow in the daytime with shimmering metallic knits. Show off your shoulders in a skinny garnet top, sparkle in a cropped gold gilet, cover up in style with a sophisticated pewter jacket, or go for allover shine in a copper sequin tank top. Slip into a dreamy, creamy cardigan decorated with the subtle sheen of pearly beads, take on a tougher look with studs and stones on denim, and accessorize your outfit with a glittering brushed wrap or sequin-scattered scarf.

Sequin knitting is slow but it's not difficult and you'll create a classic that will shine at any party.

Sequin Tank Top

MEASUREMENTS

To fit bust

in.	32	34	36	38	40	42
cm	81	86	91	97	102	107

Actual bust

in.	35	37	39	41	43	45
cm	89	94	99	104	109	114

Actual length

in.	19	19½	20¼	21	21½	22
cm	48.5	50	51.5	53.5	54.5	56

In the instructions, figures are given for the smallest size first; larger sizes follow in brackets. Where only one figure is given, this applies to all sizes.

MATERIALS

- 2 (2: 2: 2: 3: 3) × 3½ oz. (100 g) balls of Sirdar Wash 'n' Wear 4ply in Caramel, 337
- 8 (9: 10: 11: 12: 13) strands of 1,000 flat 10 mm sequins, FS10, shade 9
- Pair of size 3 (3.25 mm) knitting needles

TENSION

- 24 sts and 34 rows to 4 in. (10 cm) over sequin patt on size 3 (3.25 mm) needles. Change needle size if necessary to obtain this tension.

ABBREVIATIONS

- **pfb** – purl into front and back of st
- **sq1** – bring a sequin up close to back of work and k next st through back of loop drawing sequin through to RS as st is formed
- **[ ]** – work instructions in square brackets as directed

See also page 12.

NOTES

- Thread sequins on to the yarn before starting to knit.
- Although the sequins are flat, they do have a very slight curve. Thread the sequins with the upper side of the curve toward the ball of yarn. If your sequins are not on strands, check that they face the same way before threading them.

BACK

Cast on 95 (101: 107: 113: 119: 125) sts.

1st row: (RS) K1, [sq1, k1] to end.

2nd and 4th rows: P.

3rd row: K2, [sq1, k1] to last st, k1.

These 4 rows form the sequin patt.

Cont in patt, work 33 more rows, so ending with a 1st patt row.

Inc row: (WS) Pfb, p to last 2 sts, pfb, p1.

Cont in patt, inc in this way at each end of 5 foll 8th rows. [107 (113: 119: 125: 131: 137) sts.]

Patt 25 (27: 29: 31: 33: 35) rows, so ending with a RS row.

Shape Armholes

Cast off 5 sts at beg of next 2 rows. P 1 row.

Dec row: (RS) K2tog, patt to last 2 sts, skpo.

Cont in patt, dec in this way at each end of next 8 (9: 10: 11: 12: 13) RS rows. [79 (83: 87: 91: 95: 99) sts **.]

Patt 37 (37: 39: 41: 41: 43) rows.

Shape Neck

Next row: (RS) Patt 17 (18: 19: 20: 21: 22), turn and complete right side on these sts. P 1 row.

Dec row: (RS) Patt to last 2 sts, skpo.

Cont in patt, dec in this way at end of next RS row. [15 (16: 17: 18: 19: 20) sts.]

P 1 row. Cast off.

With RS facing, leave center 45 (47: 49: 51: 53: 55) sts on a holder, patt to end. [17 (18: 19: 20: 21: 22) sts.]

P 1 row.

Dec row: (RS) K2tog, patt to end.

Cont in patt, dec in this way at beg of next RS row. [15 (16: 17: 18: 19: 20) sts.]

P 1 row. Cast off.

FRONT

Beg 3rd patt row, work as given for back to **.

Patt 9 (9: 11: 13: 13: 15) rows.

Shape Neck

Next row: (RS) Patt 28 (29: 30: 31: 32: 33), turn and complete left side on these sts. P 1 row.

Dec row: (RS) Patt to last 2 sts, skpo.

Cont in patt, dec in this way at end of next 12 RS rows. [15 (16: 17: 18: 19: 20) sts.]

Patt 7 rows. Cast off.

With RS facing, leave center 23 (25: 27: 29: 31: 33) sts on a holder, patt to end. [28 (29: 30: 31: 32: 33) sts.] P 1 row.

Dec row: (RS) K2tog, patt to end.

Cont in patt, dec in this way at beg of next 12 RS rows. [15 (16: 17: 18: 19: 20) sts.]

Patt 7 rows. Cast off.

TO MAKE UP

Join left shoulder.

Neck edging: K up 5 sts down right back neck, patt 45 (47: 49: 51: 53: 55) sts from holder, k up 4 sts up left back neck and 24 sts down left front neck, patt 23 (25: 27: 29: 31: 33) sts from holder, k up 25 sts up right front neck. [126 (130: 134: 138: 142: 146) sts.] P 1 row.

Next row: (RS) K2, [sq1, k1] to end. Cast off knitwise.

Armhole edgings: K up 92 (96: 102: 108: 112: 118) sts around left armhole edge.

Complete as given for neck edging. Join right shoulder seam and work right armhole edging to match. Join side seams.

There are lots of different ways you can wind, twist or knot this long narrow scarf glinting with scattered sequins.

Skinny Scarf

EASY

MEASUREMENTS
- 1¼ in. (3 cm) wide × 79 in. (200 cm) long, excluding fringe

MATERIALS
- 1 oz. (25 g) ball of Rowan Kid Silk Haze in Candy Girl, 606
- Pair of size 3 (3.25 mm) knitting needles
- Flat 10 mm sequins in pink and purple
- Sewing needle with a narrow oval eye
- Medium size crochet hook

ABBREVIATIONS
- **sq1** – slide a sequin along the yarn and hold it tight against the right-hand needle, insert right-hand needle in next st, take yarn around right-hand needle to make a k st then push sequin through the st to RS as it is being slipped off the needle, tighten yarn if necessary before proceeding to next st

See also page 12.

TO BEGIN
Use sewing needle to thread sequins directly on to yarn, alternating colors.

Cast on 18 sts.

Beg k row, st-st 4 rows.

Now patt as follows:

5th row: (RS) K7, sq1, k5, sq1, k4.

Beg p row, st-st 3 rows.

9th row: K4, sq1, k5, sq1, k7.

Beg p row, st-st 3 rows, so ending with 12th row p.

5th–12th rows form patt. Repeat these 8 rows until the scarf measures 79 in. (200 cm).

K one row.

Cast off knitwise.

TO MAKE UP
RS facing, fold so that edges meet to form a tube then mattress stitch back seam, not pulling the stitches up too tightly.

Fringe

Cut 12½ in. (32 cm) lengths of yarn without
   sequins to make 10 tassels with 3 strands in
   each.
With back seam facing, insert crochet hook
   through both layers at center of one end
   of scarf, catch 3 doubled strands, and pull
   them through to make a loop. Insert the
   hook in the loop, pull the strands through
   and tighten.
Make a tassel at each corner and then fill
   the spaces between with a tassel. Tassel
   opposite end in the same way. Using
   sewing needle, thread single sequins on
   random strands of fringe and knot the
   strands to hold the sequins in place.

Cover up glamorously in a chunky jacket with dense zigzag ribs and fully-fashioned shapings.

Lurex Jacket

MEASUREMENTS

To fit bust

in.	32–34	36–38
cm	81–86	91–97

Actual bust

in.	34½	39¼
cm	88	100

Actual length

in.	18½	19¾
cm	47	50

Actual sleeve length

in.	17¾	17¾
cm	45	45

In the instructions, figures are given for the smaller size first; the larger size follows in brackets. Where only one figure is given, this applies to both sizes.

MATERIALS

- 28 (30) × 1 oz. (25 g) balls of Rowan Lurex Shimmer in Pewter, 333
- Pair of size 7 (4.5 mm) knitting needles

TENSION

- 30 sts and 28 rows to 4 in. (10 cm) over patt on size 7 (4.5 mm) needles with yarn used double.

ABBREVIATIONS

- **d inc** – double increase: k in back then front of st, insert left-hand needle point behind the vertical strand that runs downward from between the 2 sts just made and k in back of this strand, so making 3 sts from one
- **m1p** – make a st by picking up strand in front of next st and p in back of it
- **t2k** – twist 2 sts knitwise on RS rows: take needle behind first st on left-hand needle and k in back of 2nd st, k in front of first st then slip both sts off tog
- **t2p** – twist 2 sts purlwise on WS rows: take needle in front of first st on left-hand needle and p 2nd st, p first st then slip both sts off tog

For t2k and t2p, see pages 20–21. See also page 12.

NOTES

○ Yarn is used double throughout.
○ Increases and decreases are alternately single and double in order to keep the stitch pattern correct.

BACK

Cast on 154 (178) sts.
1st row: (RS) P2, * t2k, p2; rep from * to end.
2nd row: K2, * t2p, k2; rep from * to end.
Rep 1st and 2nd rows 6 times more.
15th row: (RS) P2tog, * t2k, p2tog; rep from * to end. ** [115 (133) sts.]
Now patt as follows:
1st row: (WS) K1, * t2p, k1; rep from * to end.
2nd row: P1, * t2k, p1; rep from * to end.
These 2 rows form patt. Rep 1st and 2nd patt rows 5 (7) times more, then 1st patt row again. *** **1st inc row:** (RS) P1, t2k, d inc, patt to last 4 sts, d inc, t2k, p1.
Next row: K1, t2p twice, patt to last 5 sts, t2p twice, k1. Patt 6 rows as set.
2nd inc row: (RS) P1, t2k, m1p, patt to last 3 sts, m1p, t2k, p1. Patt 7 rows. ***
Rep from *** to *** twice more. [133 (151) sts.]

Shape Armholes

Cast off 6 (9) sts at beg of next 2 rows.
1st dec row: (RS) P1, t2k, p3tog, patt to last 6 sts, p3tog, t2k, p1.
Next row: K1, t2p, k2, patt to last 5 sts, k2, t2p, k1.
2nd dec row: P1, t2k, p2tog, patt to last 5 sts, p2tog, t2k, p1.
Next row: Patt to end. **** Rep these 4 rows 3 (4) times more. [97 (103) sts.] Patt 28 rows straight.

Shape Neck

1st row: (RS) Patt 22 (25), p3tog, t2k, p1, turn.
Cont on these sts only for first side and leave rem sts on a spare needle.

○ To prevent the yarn from tangling keep a rubber band around each ball and only release a short length of yarn as required.

Cont to dec at neck edge as for armhole shaping on next 5 RS rows. [19 (22) sts.]
Patt one row, so ending with a WS row.
Cast off firmly.
Next row: (RS) Rejoin yarn to inner end of rem sts, firmly cast off center 41 sts, t2k, p3tog, patt to end.
Complete to match first side.

RIGHT FRONT
Cast on 86 (98) sts.
Work as beg of back to **. [64 (73) sts.]
Patt 13 (17) rows straight. ***

Shape Front and Side
1st row: (RS) Patt 6, p3tog, patt to last 4 sts, d inc, t2k, p1. Patt 3 rows as set.
5th row: Patt 6, p2tog, patt to end. Patt 3 rows.
9th row: Patt 6, p3tog, patt to last 3 sts, m1p, t2k, p1. Cont to dec at front edge on every foll 4th row, working alternately p2tog and p3tog, while at the same time inc at side edge on every foll 8th row, working alternate double and single incs, until a total of 6 inc rows has been completed.
Cont to shape front edge as before, patt 8 rows straight at side edge, so ending with a RS row. [53 (62) sts.]

Shape Armhole
Cast off 6 (9) sts at beg of next row.
Next row: (RS) Patt to last 6 sts, p3tog, t2k, p1.
Cont to shape front edge as before, at the same time cont to dec as back armhole until 8 (10) dec rows have been completed.

Keeping armhole edge straight, cont to dec at front edge as before until 25 (28) sts rem.
Patt straight until front matches back to shoulder, so ending with a WS row.

Neckband Extension
Next row: Patt 7 sts, turn. Cont on these sts only and leave rem 18 (21) sts on a st holder.
Patt straight until extension, slightly stretched, fits to center back neck. Cast off firmly.

Shape Shoulder
Next row: (RS) Rejoin yarn to inner end of rem 18 (21) sts, cast off firmly.

LEFT FRONT
As right front to ***.

Shape Side and Front
1st row: (RS) P1, t2k, d inc, patt to last 9 sts, p3tog, patt 6.
Cont to match right front, reversing armhole shaping by working one row less to armhole.
Cont until front matches back to shoulder, so ending with a WS row.

Neckband Extension
Next row: Cast off 18 (21) sts, patt rem 7 sts.
Complete as right neckband extension.

SLEEVES

Cast on 61 (64) sts.

1st row: (RS) P1, * t2k, p1; rep from * to end.
2nd row: K1, * t2p, k1; rep from * to end.
Rep these 2 rows 3 (7) times more.
1st inc row: (RS) P1, t2k, d inc, patt to last 4
 sts, d inc, t2k, p1. Patt 7 (5) rows as set.
2nd inc row: P1, t2k, m1p, patt to last 3 sts,
 m1p, t2k, p1.
Cont to inc in this way, alternating double
 and single inc rows, on every foll 8th (6th)
 row until a total of 14 (16) inc rows has been
 completed. [103 (112) sts.]
Patt straight until work measures 17¾ in.
 (45 cm), ending with a WS row.

Shape Top

Work as back armhole shaping to ****.
Rep last 4 rows 8 (9) times more. [37 (34) sts.]
Cast off 3 sts at beg of next 4 rows.
Firmly cast off rem 25 (22) sts.

TO MAKE UP

Join shoulder seams. Join ends of neckband
 extensions and sew inner edge around back
 neck. Set in sleeves. Join side and sleeve
 seams.

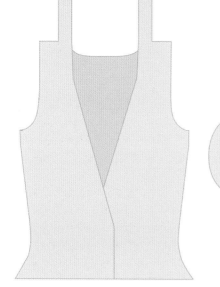

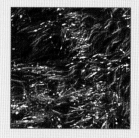

This super-soft, brushed yarn is shot through with random bursts of metallic gold giving a sophisticated effect to the simplest of knitted cover-ups.

Glitter Wrap

EASY

MEASUREMENTS

Actual width
in.   24¾
cm   63

Actual length
in.   62
cm   158

MATERIALS

- 10 × 1¾ oz. (50 g) balls of Sirdar Zanzibar in Arabia, shade 820
- Pair of size 8 (5 mm) knitting needles
- Size 8 (5 mm) circular needle, 39½ in. (100 cm) long

TENSION

- 20 sts and 26 rows to 4 in. (10 cm) over st-st on size 8 (5 mm) needles. Change needle size if necessary to obtain this tension.

ABBREVIATIONS

- [ ] – work instructions in square brackets as directed

See also page 12.

NOTES

- Checking your tension isn't easy when you can't see the stitches! Before measuring, hold your sample up to the light to count and mark the stitches, then turn it over to bump your thumbnail down the ridges to count and mark the rows.
- If you want to measure the length of the center of the wrap rather than count the rows, just remember to lie your knitting flat and spread out the stitches to the full width before measuring the length. Sirdar Zanzibar makes a floppy, flexible fabric that will stretch when held up.
- If you find that the metallic gold patches clump together, use two balls of yarn working 2 rows alternately with each to break up the patches.
- To pick up stitches evenly, divide the long edges into 6 sections and pick up 50 stitches from each section and one extra stitch from the center. Divide the short ends into two sections and pick up 54 stitches from each section and one extra stitch from the center.

○ If you want a simpler knit, just work the center without the frilled edge. You'll need only 7 balls of yarn and your wrap will measure 21½ in. (55 cm) wide and 59 in. (150 cm) long.

CENTER

Cast on 110 sts.
Beg k row, st-st 390 rows.
Cast off loosely.

EDGING

With RS facing and using circular needle, k up 301 sts along one long edge.
1st row: K.
2nd row: (RS) P3, [k1, p1] to last 4 sts, k1, p3.
3rd row: K3, [yo, p1, yo, k5] to last 4 sts, yo, p1, yo, k3.
4th row: P3, [k3, p5] to last 6 sts, k3, p3.
5th row: K3, [yo, p3, yo, k5] to last 6 sts, yo, p3, yo, k3.
6th row: P3, [k5, p5] to last 8 sts, k5, p3.
7th row: K3, [yo, p5, yo, k5] to last 8 sts, yo, p5, yo, k3.
8th row: P3, [k7, p5] to last 10 sts, k7, p3.
Cast off loosely in rib.
Work 2nd long edging in the same way. K up 109 sts along one short edge.
Work as given for first long edge.
Work 2nd short edging in the same way.

TO MAKE UP

Darn in ends. Join corner seams.

Slip on a small waistcoat that's a richly-patterned brocade of interwoven cables in fine metallic yarn.

Glimmering Vest

INTERMEDIATE

MEASUREMENTS

To fit bust

in.	32–34	36–38	40–42
cm	81–86	91–97	102–107

Actual measurement across back

in.	17¾	19¾	21½
cm	45	50	55

Actual length

in.	15	17	19¼
cm	38	43.5	49

In the instructions, figures are given for the smallest size first; larger sizes follow in brackets. Where only one figure is given, this applies to all sizes.

MATERIALS

- 10 (11: 12) × 1 oz. (25 g) balls of Rowan Lurex Shimmer in Antique White Gold, 332
- Pair each of size 1 (2.25 mm) and size 2 or 3 (3 mm) knitting needles
- Size 1 (2.25 mm) circular needle, 39½ in. (100 cm) long
- Cable needle

TENSION

- 48 sts and 43 rows to 4 in. (10 cm) over patt on size 2 or 3 (3 mm) needles.

ABBREVIATIONS

- **c4b** – sl next 2 sts on to cable needle and hold at back, k2 then k2 from cable needle
- **c4f** – as c4b but hold cable needle at front
- **c4bp** – sl next 2 sts on to cable needle and hold at back, k2 then p2 from cable needle
- **c4fp** – sl next 2 sts on to cable needle and hold at front, p2 then k2 from cable needle
- **[ ]** – work instructions in square brackets as directed

See also page 12.

BACK

Using size 1 (2.25 mm) needles, cast on 148 (164: 180) sts. K 4 rows.

Inc row: (RS) K3, kfb, * k4, [kfb] 4 times; rep from * to last 8 sts, k4, kfb, k3. ** 218 (242: 266) sts.]

Change to size 2 or 3 (3 mm) needles and patt as follows or from chart on page 87:

1st row: (WS) K1, p2, k8, * p4, k8; rep from * to last 3 sts, p2, k1.

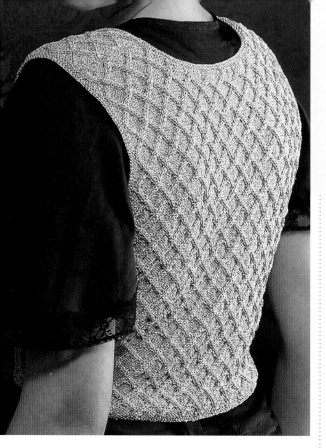

○ Patterning on every RS row requires a certain amount of dexterity so use a cranked cable needle to reduce the risk of the double pointed needle cable slipping out of the work.
○ The cable stitch pattern is given as row-by-row instructions and as a chart, so choose which method you prefer.

These 12 rows form patt. Rep 1st–12th rows 5 (6: 7) times more, then work 1st–7th rows again, so ending with a WS row.

Shape Armholes

Slipping the first st of each group of sts, cast off 3 sts at beg of next 24 (28: 32) rows. [146 (158: 170) sts.]

Cont straight until 3rd row of 13th (15th: 17th) patt has been completed, so ending with a WS row.

Shape Neck

1st row: Patt 44 (50: 56) sts, turn. Cont on these sts only for first side and leave rem sts on a spare needle.

Dec one st at neck edge on next 6 rows. [38 (44: 50) sts.]

Patt 5 rows straight, so ending with a WS row.

Cast off, working each pair of p sts as p2tog.

Next row: (RS) Rejoin yarn to inner end of rem sts, cast off center 58 sts, working each pair of p sts as p2tog, then patt to end.

Complete to match first side.

LEFT FRONT

Using size 1 (2.25 mm) needles, cast on 52 (60: 68) sts.

Work as beg of back to **. [74 (86: 98) sts.]

Change to size 2 or 3 (3 mm) needles. ***

Patt as back until 7th row of 7th (8th: 9th) patt has been completed.

2nd row: P1, k2, * p8, c4b; rep from * to last 11 sts, p8, k2, p1.

3rd row: As 1st row.

4th row: P1, * c4fp, p4, c4bp; rep from * to last st, p1.

5th and WS rows: K all k sts and p all p sts as they appear.

6th row: P3, * c4fp, c4bp, p4; rep from * to last 11 sts, c4fp, c4bp, p3.

8th row: P5, * c4f, p8; rep from * to last 9 sts, c4f, p5.

10th row: P3, * c4bp, c4fp, p4; rep from * to last 11 sts, c4bp, c4fp, p3.

12th row: P1, c4bp, * p4, c4fp, c4bp; rep from * to last 9 sts, p4, c4fp, p1.

Alternatively, work 1st–12th rows of chart, reading odd-numbered WS rows from left to right and even-numbered RS rows from right to left.

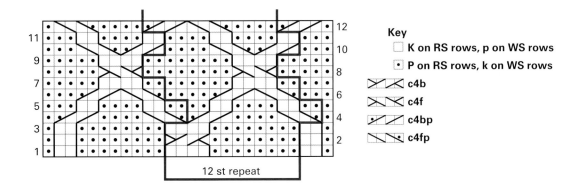

Key

☐ K on RS rows, p on WS rows

⊡ P on RS rows, k on WS rows

⟍⟍⟋ c4b

⟍⟍⟍ c4f

⟍⟍⟋ c4bp

⟍⟍⟍ c4fp

12 st repeat

Shape Armhole

Slipping first st of each group of sts, cast off 3 sts at beg of next 12 (14: 16) RS rows. [38 (44: 50) sts.]

Patt straight until work matches back to shoulder, so ending with a WS row.

Cast off, working each pair of p sts as p2tog.

RIGHT FRONT

Work as left front to ***.

Cont as back until 8th row of 7th (8th: 9th) patt has been completed.

Shape Armhole

Slipping the first st of each group of sts, cast off 3 sts at beg of next 12 (14: 16) WS rows. [38 (44: 50) sts.]

Complete to match left front.

FRONT BAND

Join shoulder seams.

With RS facing and using size 1 (2.25 mm) circular needle, pick up and k 3 sts from right front edging, 120 (138: 156) sts from edging to shoulder, 9 sts down right back neck, 40 sts across back neck, 9 sts up left back neck, 120 (138: 156) sts down left front and 3 sts from left front edging. [304 (340: 376) sts.]

K 2 rows.

Cast off knitwise.

ARMHOLE EDGING

With RS facing and using size 1 (2.25 mm) needles, pick up and k3 sts from each group of 3 cast-off sts of right back armhole, then 40 (52: 64) sts to shoulder seam, 40 (52: 64) sts down right front armhole and 3 sts from each group of 3 cast-off sts of right front armhole. [152 (188: 224) sts.]

K one row.

Next row: (RS) [K4, k2tog] 6 (7: 8) times, k to last 36 (42: 48) sts, [k2tog, k4] 6 times. [140 (174: 208) sts.]

Cast off knitwise.

Work left armhole edging to match.

TO MAKE UP

Press lightly according to ball band. Join side seams.

Get a touch of country-and-western glamour with this shaped and fitted, studded and spangled, "denim" knit.

Studded "Denim" Jacket

INTERMEDIATE

MEASUREMENTS

To fit bust

in.	32	34	36	38	40	42	44
cm	81	86	91	97	102	107	112

Actual bust

in.	33¼	35½	37½	39½	41¾	45¼	46
cm	84.5	90	95	100.5	106	115.5	117

Actual length (after washing)

in.	19	19¼	20	20¾	21¼	22	22½
cm	48	49	51	53	54	56	57

Actual sleeve length (after washing)

in.	17¾	17¾	18	18	18	18½	18½
cm	45	45	46	46	46	47	47

In the instructions, figures are given for the smallest size first; larger sizes follow in brackets. Where only one figure is given, this applies to all sizes.

MATERIALS

- 8 (9: 10: 11: 12: 13: 14) × 1¾ oz. (50 g) balls of Elle True Blue 100% Pure Indigo Dyed Cotton DK in Light Denim, shade 111
- Pair each of size 3 (3.25 mm) and size 6 (4 mm) knitting needles
- 9 buttons
- 200 white metal round, domed studs
- Assorted clear glass stones, sequins, and silvery beads
- Metallic silver sewing thread and sharp needle

TENSION

- 22 sts and 30 rows to 4 in. (10 cm) over st-st, before washing, on size 6 (4 mm) needles. Change needle size if necessary to obtain this tension.

ABBREVIATIONS

- **m-st** – moss stitch
- **pfb** – purl into front and back of st
- **[ ]** – work instructions in square brackets as directed

See also page 12.

○ You can play around with the spacing of the studs by pushing them into the knitting. The prongs will hold them in place but they can easily be moved. When you're happy with the effect, use needle nose pliers, tweezers, or the end of a metal nail file to bend the prongs in over the yarn on the wrong side.

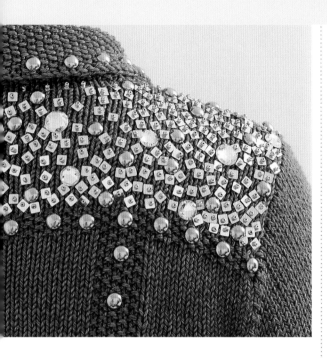

NOTE

○ Elle True Blue Indigo Dyed Cotton DK is designed to fade and shrinks by 5% in length after the first wash. The instructions allow for this.

BACK

Using size 3 (3.25 mm) needles, cast on 83 (89: 95: 101: 107: 113: 119) sts.

1st row: (RS) P1, [k1, p1] to end.

This row forms m-st. M-st 7 more rows.

Change to size 6 (4 mm) needles.

1st row: (RS) M-st 5, k13 (15: 17: 19: 21: 23: 25), m-st 5, k37 (39: 41: 43: 45: 47: 49), m-st 5, k13 (15: 17: 19: 21: 23: 25), m-st 5.

2nd row: M-st 5, p13 (15: 17: 19: 21: 23: 25), m-st 5, p37 (39: 41: 43: 45: 47: 49), m-st 5, p13 (15: 17: 19: 21: 23: 25), m-st 5.

These 2 rows form st-st at center and sides with 5 sts in m-st between panels and at vent edges. Work 8 more rows.

Vent Tops

1st row: (RS) M-st 3, k15 (17: 19: 21: 23: 25: 27), m-st 5, k37 (39: 41: 43: 45: 47: 49), m-st 5, k15 (17: 19: 21: 23: 25: 27), m-st 3.

2nd row: P1, k1, p16 (18: 20: 22: 24: 26: 28), m-st 5, p37 (39: 41: 43: 45: 47: 49), m-st 5, p16 (18: 20: 22: 24: 26: 28), k1, p1.

3rd row: P1, k17 (19: 21: 23: 25: 27: 29), m-st 5, k37 (39: 41: 43: 45: 47: 49), m-st 5, k17 (19: 21: 23: 25: 27: 29), p1.

4th row: Pfb, p17 (19: 21: 23: 25: 27: 29), m-st 5, p37 (39: 41: 43: 45: 47: 49), m-st 5, p17 (19: 21: 23: 25: 27: 29), pfb. [85 (91: 97: 103: 109: 115: 121) sts.]

Next row: K19 (21: 23: 25: 27: 29: 31), m-st 5, k37 (39: 41: 43: 45: 47: 49), m-st 5, k19 (21: 23: 25: 27: 29: 31).

Cont in st-st with 5 sts in m-st between panels, work 5 rows.

1st dec row: (RS) K2, k2tog, k12 (14: 16: 18: 20: 22: 24), skpo, k1, m-st 5, k37 (39: 41: 43: 45: 47: 49), m-st 5, k1, k2tog, k12 (14: 16: 18: 20: 22: 24), skpo, k2. [81 (87: 93: 99: 105: 111: 117) sts.]

Work 5 rows.

2nd dec row: (RS) K2, k2tog, k10 (12: 14: 16: 18: 20: 22), skpo, k1, m-st 5, k37 (39: 41: 43: 45: 47: 49), m-st 5, k1, k2tog, k10 (12: 14: 16: 18: 20: 22), skpo, k2. [77 (83: 89: 95: 101: 107: 113) sts.]

Work 11 rows.

1st inc row: (RS) K1, kfb, k11 (13: 15: 17: 19: 21: 23), kfb, k1, m-st 5, k37 (39: 41: 43: 45:

- The sequins on the yoke are square but round sequins would work just as well.
- If your jeans have brass buttons, decorate your jacket with studs, stones, and sequins in yellow metal shades of copper, brass, and gold.
- For a smoother line, slip the first stitch of each cast-off group when shaping the sleeve top.

47: 49), m-st 5, kfb, k11 (13: 15: 17: 19: 21: 23), kfb, k2. [81 (87: 93: 99: 105: 111: 117) sts.]
Work 7 rows.

2nd inc row: (RS) K1, kfb, k13 (15: 17: 19: 21: 23: 25), kfb, k1, m-st 5, k37 (39: 41: 43: 45: 47: 49), m-st 5, kfb, k13 (15: 17: 19: 21: 23: 25), kfb, k2. [85 (91: 97: 103: 109: 115: 121) sts.]
Work 7 rows.

3rd inc row: (RS) K1, kfb, k15 (17: 19: 21: 23: 25: 27), kfb, k1, m-st 5, k37 (39: 41: 43: 45: 47: 49), m-st 5, kfb, k15 (17: 19: 21: 23: 25: 27), kfb, k2. [89 (95: 101: 107: 113: 119: 125) sts.]
Work 7 rows.

4th inc row: (RS) K1, kfb, k17 (19: 21: 23: 25: 27: 29), kfb, k1, m-st 5, k37 (39: 41: 43: 45: 47: 49), m-st 5, kfb, k17 (19: 21: 23: 25: 27: 29), kfb, k2. [93 (99: 105: 111: 117: 123: 129) sts.]
Work 27 (29: 29: 31: 31: 33: 33) rows.

Shape Armholes

Cast off 4 (5: 5: 6: 6: 7: 7) sts at beg of next 2 rows.
Dec row: K3, k2tog, patt to last 5 sts, skpo, k3.
Dec in this way at each end of next 3 (4: 5: 6: 7: 8: 9) RS rows. [77 (79: 83: 85: 89: 91: 95) sts.]
Work 17 (17: 19: 21: 23: 25: 25) rows.

Yoke

Change to size 3 (3.25 mm) needles. Beg k1 (k1: p1: p1: k1: k1: p1), m-st 5 rows.
Change to size 6 (4 mm) needles. Beg p row, st-st 25 (25: 27: 27: 27: 27: 27) rows.

Shape Shoulders

Cast off 8 (9: 9: 10: 10: 11: 11) sts at beg of next 2 rows and 9 (9: 10: 10: 11: 11: 12) sts at beg of foll 2 rows. [43 (43: 45: 45: 47: 47: 49) sts.]
Cast off.

LEFT FRONT

Using size 3 (3.25 mm) needles, cast on 44 (47: 50: 53: 56: 59: 62) sts.
Ending RS rows and beg WS rows k1 for 1st, 3rd, 5th, and 7th sizes, m-st 8 rows as given for back. Change to size 6 (4 mm) needles.

1st row: (RS) M-st 5, k13 (15: 17: 19: 21: 23: 25), m-st 5, k16 (17: 18: 19: 20: 21: 22), m-st 5.
2nd row: M-st 5, p16 (17: 18: 19: 20: 21: 22), m-st 5, p13 (15: 17: 19: 21: 23: 25), m-st 5.
These 2 rows form st-st at center and side with 5 sts in m-st at vent edging, between panels and at front edge for band. Work 8 more rows.

Vent Top

1st row: (RS) M-st 3, k15 (17: 19: 21: 23: 25: 27), m-st 5, k16 (17: 18: 19: 20: 21: 22), m-st 5.
2nd row: M-st 5, p16 (17: 18: 19: 20: 21: 22), m-st 5, p16 (18: 20: 22: 24: 26: 28), k1, p1.
3rd row: P1, k17 (19: 21: 23: 25: 27: 29), m-st 5, k16 (17: 18: 19: 20: 21: 22), m-st 5.
4th row: M-st 5, p16 (17: 18: 19: 20: 21: 22), m-st 5, p17 (19: 21: 23: 25: 27: 29), pfb. [45 (48: 51: 54: 57: 60: 63) sts.]
Next row: K19 (21: 23: 25: 27: 29: 31), m-st 5, k16 (17: 18: 19: 20: 21: 22), m-st 5.
Cont in st-st with 5 sts in m-st between panels and at front edge, work 5 rows.

1st dec row: (RS) K2, k2tog, k12 (14: 16: 18: 20: 22: 24), skpo, k1, m-st 5, k16 (17: 18: 19: 20: 21: 22), m-st 5. [43 (46: 49: 52: 55: 58: 61) sts.]
Work 5 rows.

2nd dec row: (RS) K2, k2tog, k10 (12: 14: 16: 18: 20: 22), skpo, k1, m-st 5, k16 (17: 18: 19: 20: 21: 22), m-st 5. [41 (44: 47: 50: 53: 56: 59) sts.]
Work 11 rows.

1st inc row: (RS) K1, kfb, k11 (13: 15: 17: 19: 21: 23), kfb, k1, m-st 5, k16 (17: 18: 19: 20: 21: 22), m-st 5. [43 (46: 49: 52: 55: 58: 61) sts.]
Work 7 rows.

2nd inc row: (RS) K1, kfb, k13 (15: 17: 19: 21: 23: 25), kfb, k1, m-st 5, k16 (17: 18: 19: 20: 21: 22), m-st 5. [45 (48: 51: 54: 57: 60: 63) sts.]
Work 7 rows.

3rd inc row: (RS) K1, kfb, k15 (17: 19: 21: 23: 25: 27), kfb, k1, m-st 5, k16 (17: 18: 19: 20: 21: 22), m-st 5. [47 (50: 53: 56: 59: 62: 65) sts.]
Work 7 rows.

4th inc row: (RS) K1, kfb, k17 (19: 21: 23: 25: 27: 29), kfb, k1, m-st 5, k16 (17: 18: 19: 20: 21: 22), m-st 5. [49 (52: 55: 58: 61: 64: 67) sts.]
Work 27 (29: 29: 31: 31: 33: 33) rows.

Shape Armhole

Cast off 4 (5: 5: 6: 6: 7: 7) sts at beg of next row.
Patt 1 row.

Dec row: (RS) K3, k2tog, patt to end.
Dec in this way at beg of next 3 (4: 5: 6: 7: 8: 9) RS rows. [41 (42: 44: 45: 47: 48: 50) sts.]
Work 17 (17: 19: 21: 23: 25: 25) rows.

Yoke

Change to size 3 (3.25 mm) needles. Beg k1 (k1: p1: p1: k1: k1: p1), m-st 5 rows.
Change to size 6 (4 mm) needles.

Next row: (WS) M-st 5, p to end.

Next row: K to last 5 sts, m-st 5.
Cont in st-st with m-st 5 for band, work 7 rows.

Shape Neck

1st row: (RS) K31 (32: 33: 34: 35: 36: 37), turn and leave 10 (10: 11: 11: 12: 12: 13) sts on a holder for neck.

2nd row: Slipping first st, cast off 2 sts, p to end.

3rd row: K to last 2 sts, skpo.
Work 2nd and 3rd rows 3 more times, then work 2nd row again. [17 (18: 19: 20: 21: 22: 23) sts.] St-st 6 (6: 8: 8: 8: 8: 8) rows, so ending with a p row.

Shape Shoulder

Cast off 8 (9: 9: 10: 10: 11: 11) sts at beg of next row and 9 (9: 10: 10: 11: 11: 12) sts at beg of foll RS row.
Place markers for 8 buttons on WS rows, the top one in line with the band of moss stitch across the yoke, the lowest about 3½ in. (9 cm) from lower edge, with 6 more spaced evenly between. The 9th buttonhole will be in the collar.

RIGHT FRONT

Using size 3 (3.25 mm) needles, cast on 44 (47: 50: 53: 56: 59: 62) sts.
Beg RS rows and ending WS rows k1 for 1st, 3rd, 5th, and 7th sizes, m-st 8 rows as given for back. Change to size 6 (4 mm) needles.

1st row: (RS) M-st 5, k16 (17: 18: 19: 20: 21: 22), m-st 5, k13 (15: 17: 19: 21: 23: 25), m-st 5.

2nd row: M-st 5, p13 (15: 17: 19: 21: 23: 25), m-st 5, p16 (17: 18: 19: 20: 21: 22), m-st 5.
These 2 rows form st-st at center and side with 5 sts in m-st at vent edging, between panels and at front edge for band. Work 8 more rows.

Vent Top

1st row: (RS) M-st 5, k16 (17: 18: 19: 20: 21: 22), m-st 5, k15 (17: 19: 21: 23: 25: 27), m-st 3.

2nd row: P1, k1, p16 (18: 20: 22: 24: 26: 28), m-st 5, p16 (17: 18: 19: 20: 21: 22), m-st 5.

3rd row: M-st 5, k16 (17: 18: 19: 20: 21: 22), m-st 5, k17 (19: 21: 23: 25: 27: 29), p1.

4th row: Pfb, p17 (19: 21: 23: 25: 27: 29), m-st 5, p16 (17: 18: 19: 20: 21: 22), m-st 5. [45 (48: 51: 54: 57: 60: 63) sts.]

Next row: M-st 5, k16 (17: 18: 19: 20: 21: 22), m-st 5, k19 (21: 23: 25: 27: 29: 31).

Cont in st-st with 5 sts in m-st between panels and at front edge, work 5 rows.

Cont as given making buttonholes opposite markers.

Buttonhole row: (WS) Patt to last 5 sts, p1, k1, yo, skpo, p1.

1st dec row: (RS) M-st 5, k16 (17: 18: 19: 20: 21: 22), m-st 5, k1, k2tog, k12 (14: 16: 18: 20: 22: 24), skpo, k2. [43 (46: 49: 52: 55: 58: 61) sts.]

Work 5 rows.

2nd dec row: (RS) M-st 5, k16 (17: 18: 19: 20: 21: 22), m-st 5, k1, k2tog, k10 (12: 14: 16: 18: 20: 22), skpo, k2. [41 (44: 47: 50: 53: 56: 59) sts.]

Work 11 rows.

1st inc row: (RS) M-st 5, k16 (17: 18: 19: 20: 21: 22), m-st 5, kfb, k11 (13: 15: 17: 19: 21: 23), kfb, k2. [43 (46: 49: 52: 55: 58: 61) sts.]

Work 7 rows.

2nd inc row: (RS) M-st 5, k16 (17: 18: 19: 20: 21: 22), m-st 5, kfb, k13 (15: 17: 19: 21: 23: 25), kfb, k2. [45 (48: 51: 54: 57: 60: 63) sts.]

Work 7 rows.

3rd inc row: (RS) M-st 5, k16 (17: 18: 19: 20: 21: 22), m-st 5, kfb, k15 (17: 19: 21: 23: 25: 27), kfb, k2. [47 (50: 53: 56: 59: 62: 65) sts.]

Work 7 rows.

4th inc row: (RS) M-st 5, k16 (17: 18: 19: 20: 21: 22), m-st 5, kfb, k17 (19: 21: 23: 25: 27: 29), kfb, k2. [49 (52: 55: 58: 61: 64: 67) sts.]

Work 28 (30: 30: 32: 32: 34: 34) rows.

Shape Armhole

Cast off 4 (5: 5: 6: 6: 7: 7) sts at beg of next row.

Dec row: (RS) Patt to last 5 sts, skpo, k3.

Dec in this way at end of next 3 (4: 5: 6: 7: 8: 9) RS rows. [41 (42: 44: 45: 47: 48: 50) sts.]

Work 17 (17: 19: 21: 23: 25: 25) rows.

Yoke

Change to size 3 (3.25 mm) needles. M-st 5 rows.

Change to size 6 (4 mm) needles.

Next row: (WS) P to last 5 sts, m-st 5.

Next row: M-st 5, k to end.

Cont in st-st with m-st 5 for band, work 7 rows.

Shape Neck

1st row: (RS) M-st 5, k5 (5: 6: 6: 7: 7: 8) and leave these 10 (10: 11: 11: 12: 12: 13) sts on a holder for neck, k to end. [31 (32: 33: 34: 35: 36: 37) sts.]

2nd row: P to last 2 sts, p2tog.

3rd row: Slipping first st, cast off 2 sts, k to end.

Work 2nd and 3rd rows 3 more times, then work 2nd row again.

Next row: (RS) K2tog, k to end. [17 (18: 19: 20: 21: 22: 23) sts.]

St-st 6 (6: 8: 8: 8: 8: 8) rows, so ending with a k row.

Shape Shoulder

Cast off 8 (9: 9: 10: 10: 11: 11) sts at beg of next row and 9 (9: 10: 10: 11: 11: 12) sts at beg of foll WS row.

SLEEVES

Using size 3 (3.25 mm) needles, cast on 47 (49: 49: 51: 53: 53: 55) sts. M-st 8 rows as back. Change to size 6 (4 mm) needles. Beg k row, st-st 10 rows.

Inc row: (RS) K1, kfb, k to last 3 sts, kfb, k2.

Cont in st-st, inc in this way at each end of 8 (9: 11: 13: 14: 16: 17) foll 10th (10th: 10th: 8th: 8th: 6th: 6th) rows. [65 (69: 73: 79: 83: 87: 91) sts.]

St-st until sleeve measures 18¾ (18¾: 19: 19: 19: 19½: 19½) in., 47.5 (47.5: 48.5: 48.5: 48.5: 49.5: 49.5) cm, ending with a p row.

Shape Top

Cast off 4 (5: 5: 6: 6: 7: 7) sts at beg of next 2 rows.

Dec row: K1, k2tog, patt to last 3 sts, skpo, k1.

Dec in this way at each end of next 3 (4: 5: 6: 7: 8: 9) RS rows. [49 (49: 51: 53: 55: 55: 57) sts.]

St-st 5 (5: 7: 7: 7: 9: 9) rows. Dec as before at each end of next 8 RS rows. [33 (33: 35: 37: 39: 39: 41) sts.] P 1 row.

Cast off 2 sts at beg of next 4 rows and 4 sts at beg of foll 2 rows. [17 (17: 19: 21: 23: 23: 25) sts.]

Cast off.

COLLAR

Join shoulders. Using size 3 (3.25 mm) needles, slip 10 (10: 11: 11: 12: 12: 13) sts from right front holder, k up 23 (23: 25: 25: 25: 25: 25) sts up right front neck, 43 (43: 45: 45: 47: 47: 49) sts across back neck and 23 (23: 25: 25: 25: 25: 25) sts down left front neck, k5 (5: 6: 6: 7: 7: 8), m-st 5 from holder. [109 (109: 117: 117: 121: 121: 125) sts.]

1st row: (RS) [P1, k1] to last 3 sts, yo, skpo, p1.

2nd row: P1, [k1, p1] to end.

This row forms m-st.

3rd row: Cast off 4 sts knitwise, m-st to end.

4th row: Cast off 4 sts purlwise, m-st to end. [101 (101: 109: 109: 113: 113: 117) sts.]

Cont in m-st until collar measures 4 in. (10 cm), ending with a RS row. Cast off loosely in m-st.

TO MAKE UP

Easing to fit, set in sleeves. Overlap front bands and tack to secure in place. Wash and dry jacket. Take out tacking stitches. Set studs in rows spaced evenly along m-st between panels, across each side of yoke, at lower edge of sleeves, and around collar. Scatter remaining studs at random over yoke. Using metallic yarn, sew on glass stones between studs, then fill in spaces between studs and stones with sequins. To hold each sequin in place, bring the needle up at the center hole, thread on a small bead, take the needle back through the hole, and secure on the wrong side.

Join side seams to top of vents and sleeve seams. Sew on buttons.

Add lots of pearly beads and sequins to a simple cardigan and create an enduring classic.

Beaded Cardigan

INTERMEDIATE

MEASUREMENTS

To fit bust

in.	32	34	36	38	40	42
cm	81	86	91	97	102	107

Actual bust

in.	33½	35½	37¾	39¾	41½	44
cm	85	90	96	101	107	112

Actual length

in.	19¾	20½	20¾	21½	22½	22¾
cm	50	52	53	55	57	58

Actual sleeve length

in.	17¾	17¾	17¾	17¾	17¾	17¾
cm	45	45	45	45	45	45

In the instructions, figures are given for the smallest size first; larger sizes follow in brackets. Where only one figure is given, this applies to all sizes.

MATERIALS

- 8 (8: 9: 9: 10: 10) × 1¾ oz. (50 g) balls Rowan RYC Cashsoft DK in Cream, 00500
- Pair each of size 2 (3 mm), size 3 (3.25 mm), size 5 (3.75 mm), and size 6 (4 mm) knitting needles
- Beads and sequins – 10 large beads, a quantity of medium and small pearl beads, cup sequins, and bugle beads
- Fine sewing needles and sewing thread to match the knitting yarn
- Hooks and eyes

TENSION

- 22 sts and 29 rows to 4 in. (10 cm) over st-st on size 6 (4 mm) needles.

ABBREVIATIONS

- [ ] – work instructions in square brackets the number of times stated

See also page 12.

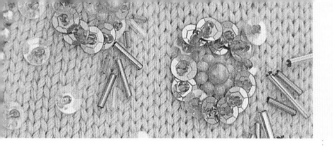

○ Don't worry if you can't find beads and sequins exactly like the ones shown—almost any mix of pearl and pale gold colors will work with this soft cream yarn.

BACK

Using size 3 (3.25 mm) needles, cast on 90 (96: 102: 108: 114: 120) sts.

Beg k row, st-st 4 rows.

P next row to mark hemline.

Change to size 5 (3.75 mm) needles and beg p row, st-st 5 rows. **

Change to size 6 (4 mm) needles.

Dec row: (RS) K1, skpo, k to last 3 sts, k2tog, k1.

Cont to dec in this way at each end of every foll 6th row until a total of 4 dec rows has been completed. [82 (88: 94: 100: 106: 112) sts.]

Beg p row, st-st 9 rows.

Inc row: (RS) K2, m1, k to last 2 sts, m1, k2.

Cont to inc in this way at each end of every foll 10th row until a total of 6 inc rows has been completed. [94 (100: 106: 112: 118: 124) sts.]

Beg and ending p row, st-st 7 (9: 11: 13: 15: 17) rows straight.

Shape Armholes

Cast off 5 (5: 5: 6: 6: 6) sts at beg of next 2 rows, then dec as for beg of back at each end of next 8 (9: 10: 10: 11: 12) RS rows. [68 (72: 76: 80: 84: 88) sts.]

Beg p row, st-st 25 (27: 27: 29: 31: 31) rows straight.

Shape Neck

1st row: (RS) K21 (23: 24: 26: 27: 29), k2tog, k1, turn.

Cont on these sts only for first side and leave rem sts on a spare needle.

2nd row: P.

3rd row: K to last 3 sts, k2tog, k1.

Rep 2nd and 3rd rows 4 times more.

P one row.

Leave rem 18 (20: 21: 23: 24: 26) sts on a spare needle.

Next row: (RS) Sl center 20 (20: 22: 22: 24: 24) sts on to a spare needle, rejoin yarn to inner end of rem sts, k1, skpo, k to end.

Complete to match first side.

LEFT FRONT

Using size 3 (3.25 mm) needles, cast on 43 (46: 49: 52: 55: 58) sts.

1st row: K to last 2 sts, kfb, k1.

2nd row: P.

Rep 1st and 2nd rows once. [45 (48: 51: 54: 57: 60) sts.]

P next row to mark hemline.

Change to size 5 (3.75 mm) needles and beg p row, st-st 5 rows.

Change to size 6 (4 mm) needles.

Dec row: (RS) K1, skpo, k to end.

Cont to dec in this way at beg of every foll 6th row until a total of 4 dec rows has been completed. [41 (44: 47: 50: 53: 56) sts.]

Beg p row, st-st 9 rows.

Inc row: (RS) K2, m1, k to end.

Cont to inc in this way at beg of every foll 10th row until a total of 6 inc rows has been completed. [47 (50: 53: 56: 59: 62) sts.]

Beg and ending p row, st-st 7 (9: 11: 13: 15: 17) rows straight.

Shape Armhole

Cast off 5 (5: 5: 6: 6: 6) sts at beg of next row.
P one row.

Next row: (RS) K1, skpo, k to end.

Cont to dec in this way at beg of next 7 (8: 9: 9: 10: 11) RS rows. [34 (36: 38: 40: 42: 44) sts.]

Beg and ending p row, st-st 17 (19: 19: 21: 23: 23) rows straight.

Shape Neck

1st row: (RS) K21 (23: 24: 26: 27: 29), k2tog, k1, turn.

Cont on these sts only and leave rem 10 (10: 11: 11: 12: 12) sts on a st holder.

Dec as for first side of back neck on next 5 RS rows. [18 (20: 21: 23: 24: 26) sts.]

Beg and ending p row, st-st 9 rows straight.

Leave sts on a spare needle.

RIGHT FRONT

Using size 3 (3.25 mm) needles, cast on 43 (46: 49: 52: 55: 58) sts.

1st row: Kfb, k to end.

2nd row: P.

Rep 1st and 2nd rows once. [45 (48: 51: 54: 57: 60) sts.]

P next row to mark hemline.

Change to size 5 (3.75 mm) needles and beg p row, st-st 5 rows.

Change to size 6 (4 mm) needles.

Dec row: (RS) K to last 3 sts, k2tog, k1.

Cont to match left front, working one more row to armhole shaping and working each armhole dec as k2tog. [34 (36: 38: 40: 42: 44) sts.]

Beg and ending p row, st-st 17 (19: 19: 21: 23: 23) rows straight.

Shape Neck

1st row: (RS) Break yarn, sl first 10 (10: 11: 11: 12: 12) sts on to a st holder, rejoin yarn at inner edge of rem sts, k1, skpo, k to end.

Complete to match left front.

SLEEVES

Using size 3 (3.25 mm) needles, cast on 46
  (48: 50: 52: 54: 56) sts.
Work as beg of back to **.
Change to size 6 (4 mm) needles.
Beg k row, st-st 10 (6: 0: 10: 4: 0) rows.
Next row: (RS) K2, m1, k to last 2 sts, m1, k2.
Cont to inc in this way on every foll 10th
  (10th: 10th: 8th: 8th: 8th) row until a total
  of 11 (12: 13: 14: 15: 16) inc rows has been
  completed. [68 (72: 76: 80: 84: 88) sts.]
St-st straight until work measures 17¾ in.
  (45 cm) from hem line, ending p row.

Shape Top

Cast off 5 (5: 5: 6: 6: 6) sts at beg of next 2
  rows then dec as for back armhole at each
  end of next 8 (9: 10: 10: 11: 12) RS rows. [42
  (44: 46: 48: 50: 52) sts.]
Dec as before at each end of next 3 (3: 3: 4: 4:
  4) alternate RS rows. [36 (38: 40: 40: 42: 44)
  sts.]
Dec as before at each end of next 3 RS rows.
  [30 (32: 34: 34: 36: 38) sts.]
Cast off 2 sts at beg of next 4 rows.
Cast off purlwise rem 22 (24: 26: 26: 28: 30)
  sts.

NECK FACING

Join shoulder seams by casting off tog sts of
  front and back shoulders: with RS tog and
  using size 6 (4 mm) needles, k tog one st
  from front shoulder and one st from back
  shoulder each time.
With RS facing and using size 3 (3.25 mm)
  needles, k10 (10: 11: 11: 12: 12) sts from right
  front neck, pick up and k18 sts to shoulder
  and 12 sts down right back neck, k20 (20: 22:
  22: 24: 24) sts from back neck, pick up and k
  12 sts up left back neck and 18 sts down left
  front neck, k10 (10: 11: 11: 12: 12) sts from left
  front neck. [100 (100: 104: 104: 112: 112) sts.]
K 2 rows.

3rd row: P2tog tbl, p to last 2 sts, p2tog.

4th row: K9 (9: 10: 10: 11: 11), m1, [k3, m1] 10 times, k20 (20: 22: 22: 24: 24), m1, [k3, m1] 10 times, k9 (9: 10: 10: 11: 11).

5th row: As 3rd row.

Cast off.

FRONT FACINGS

With RS facing and using size 3 (3.25 mm) needles, pick up and k96 (100: 104: 108: 112: 116) sts from hemline to neck facing on right front. K2 rows.

3rd row: P2tog tbl, p to last 2 sts, p2tog.

4th row: K.

5th row: As 3rd row.

Cast off.

Work left front facing to match.

TO BEAD AND MAKE UP

Press according to instructions on ball band. Turn hems and facings to wrong side, press and catch down, joining mitred corners at neck and lower fronts.

Using stitches and rows as a guide, sew medium-size pearl beads along all edges (see page 22 for how to sew on beads).

With contrast yarn count rows and stitches to tack a grid of squares to act as a guide on the part of the fronts to be beaded. Arrange the centers of 5 "flowers" on one front, placing a large pearl bead in the center and 8 smaller ones around (see the image on page 99). Stitch these in place, then use the grid to make the same arrangement on the opposite front and stitch this in place. Each time arranging and stitching a component on one front before matching it on the other, make a ring of cup sequins close together around each flower center and hold them in place with a tiny bead (see page 22). Sequins look livelier if the tones and colors are mixed and any translucent ones are used in pairs, one on top of another. Now scatter bugle beads near the flowers and cup sequins in the resulting spaces, becoming fewer around the back of the neck.

Set in sleeves. Join side and sleeve seams and hems with mattress stitch (see page 23) worked on the RS. Press seams.

Finally, sew pairs of hooks and eyes to the front facings, a little way in from the edge.

Walk tall in this lean edge-to-edge fingertip-length coat that's knitted in a soft lightweight yarn with a subtle gleam.

Cardigan Coat

MEASUREMENTS

To fit bust

in.	32–34	36–38	40–42
cm	81–86	91–97	102–107

Actual bust

in.	36	39½	43
cm	91.5	100.5	109

Actual length

in.	29½	30¼	31¼
cm	75	77	79.5

Actual sleeve length

in.	17¾	17¾	17¾
cm	45	45	45

In the instructions, figures are given for the smallest size first; larger sizes follow in brackets. Where only one figure is given, this applies to all sizes.

MATERIALS

o 10 (11: 12) × 1¾ oz. (50 g) balls of Rowan RYC Soft Lux in Powder, 002
o Pair of size 7 (4.5 mm) knitting needles

TENSION

o 18 sts and 32 rows to 4 in. (10 cm) over m-st on size 7 (4.5 mm) needles.

ABBREVIATIONS

o **d inc** – k in front, back and front of st to makev3 sts from one
o **m-st** – moss stitch
See also page 12.

BACK

Cast on 95 (103: 111) sts.
1st row: (RS) K1, * p1, k1; rep from * to end.
  This row forms m-st. Rep first row 19 times more.
21st row: (RS) K2tog, m-st to last 2 sts, skpo.
Keeping m-st correct, dec in this way at each end of every foll 20th row until a total of 6 dec rows has been completed. [83 (91: 99) sts.]
M-st straight until work measures 21½ (22: 22½) in., 55 (56: 57) cm, ending with a WS row.

○ When joining new yarn on the fronts do this at the side and not the front edges, so that the ends can be darned into a seam.

Shape Armholes

Cast off 3 (4: 5) sts at beg of next 2 rows, then dec 1 st at each end of next 7 (8: 9) RS rows. [63 (67: 71) sts.]

M-st 39 (41: 43) rows straight, so ending with a WS row.

Shape Neck

1st row: M-st 21 (23: 23) sts, turn. Cont on these sts only for first side and leave rem sts on a spare needle.

2nd row: M-st.

3rd row: M-st to last 6 sts, p3tog, k1, p1, k1. Cont to dec in this way on next 2 RS rows. [15 (17: 17) sts.]

M-st 3 rows.

Cast off in m-st.

Next row: (RS) Rejoin yarn to inner end of rem sts, cast off center 21 (21: 25) sts, m-st to end. [21 (23: 23) sts.]

M-st one row.

Next row: (RS) K1, p1, k1, p3tog, m-st to end. Cont to dec in this way on next 2 RS rows. [15 (17: 17) sts.]

M-st 3 rows.

Cast off in m-st.

LEFT FRONT

Cast on 43 (47: 51) sts.

M-st 2 rows. **

3rd row: (RS) M-st to last 3 sts, d inc, p1, k1.

M-st 3 rows.

7th row: As 3rd row. [47 (51: 55) sts.]

M-st 13 rows.

21st row: K2tog, m-st to end.

Cont to dec in this way at beg of every foll 20th row until a total of 6 dec rows has been completed. [41 (45: 49) sts.]

M-st straight until work matches back to
armhole shaping, so ending with a WS row.

Shape Armhole

Cast off 3 (4: 5) sts at beg of next row.
Dec one st at beg of next 7 (8: 9) RS rows. [31
(33: 35) sts.]
M-st 19 (21: 23) rows straight, so ending with
a WS row.

Shape Neck

1st dec row: M-st to last 6 sts, p3tog, k1, p1,
k1.
M-st 2 rows.
Next row: (WS) Cast off in m-st 8 (8: 10) sts,
m-st to end.
2nd dec row: As 1st dec row. Cont to dec in
this way at end of next 2 RS rows. [15 (17:
17) sts.]
M-st 21 rows straight.
Cast off in m-st.

RIGHT FRONT

As left front to **.
3rd row: (RS) K1, p1, d inc, m-st to end.
M-st 3 rows.
7th row: As 3rd row. [47 (51: 55) sts.]
M-st 13 rows straight.
21st row: (RS) M-st to last 2 sts, skpo.
Cont to match left front, working one more
row to armhole, so ending with a RS row.

Shape Armhole

Cast off 3 (4: 5) sts at beg of next row, then
dec one st at end of next 7 (8: 9) RS rows.
[31 (33: 35) sts.]
M-st 19 (21: 23) rows straight, so ending with
a WS row.

Shape Neck

1st dec row: K1, p1, k1, p3tog, m-st to end.
M-st one row.

Next row: (RS) Cast off 8 (8: 10) sts, m-st to end.

M-st one row.

2nd dec row: As 1st dec row.

Cont to dec in this way at beg of next 2 RS rows. [15 (17: 17) sts.]

M-st 21 rows straight.

Cast off in m-st.

SLEEVES

Cast on 43 (45: 47) sts.

M-st 16 (6: 6) rows.

Next row: (RS) K1, m1, m-st to last st, m1, k1.

Keeping m-st correct, cont to inc in this way at each end of every foll 16th (16th: 14th) row until a total of 8 (9: 10) inc rows has been completed. [59 (63: 67) sts.]

M-st straight until work measures 17¾ in. (45 cm) ending with a WS row.

Top Shaping

Cast off 3 (4: 5) sts at beg of next 2 rows.

Next row: (RS) K2tog, m-st to last 2 sts, skpo.

Cont to dec in this way on next 6 (7: 8) RS rows. [39 sts.]

Dec in this way at each end of next 4 alternate RS rows. [31 sts.]

Dec in this way at each end of next 7 RS rows.

Cast off rem 17 sts in m-st.

TO MAKE UP

Carefully pinning out rounded corners on fronts, press according to instructions on ball band. Join shoulder seams. Set in sleeves. Join side and sleeve seams.

Shine softly in a close-fitting ribbed tube with a little lace patterned bib front.

Lace Panel Top

MEASUREMENTS

To fit bust

in.	32	34	36	38
cm	81	86	91	97

Actual size, stretched

in.	32	34	36	38
cm	81	86	91	97

Actual length to underarm

in.	8½	9	9½	10
cm	22	23	24	25

In the instructions, figures are given for the smallest size first; larger sizes follow in brackets. Where only one figure is given, this applies to all sizes.

MATERIALS

- 5 (5: 6: 6) × 1 oz. (25 g) balls Rowan Lurex Shimmer in Claret, 331
- Pair of size 1 (2.25 mm) knitting needles
- 35½ in. (90 cm) narrow ribbon

TENSION

- 33 sts and 42 rows to 4 in. (10 cm) over stretched rib on size 1 (2.25 mm) needles.

ABBREVIATIONS

- **sk2po** – sl one st knitwise, k 2 tog, pass slipped st over
- **tbl** – through the back of the loop

See also page 12.

BACK

Cast on 113 (123: 131: 141) sts.

1st row: (RS) P1, * k1tbl, p1; rep from * to end.

2nd row: K1, * p1tbl, k1; rep from * to end.

These 2 rows form rib. Rep 1st and 2nd rows 4 times more.

11th row: (RS) P1, k1tbl, m1, rib to last 2 sts, m1, k1tbl, p1.

12th row: K1, p1tbl twice, rib to last 3 sts, p1tbl twice, k1.

13th row: P1, k1tbl twice, rib to last 3 sts, k1tbl twice, p1.

Rep 12th and 13th rows 5 times more, then work 12th row again.

25th row: As 11th row.

Keeping rib correct, inc one st at each end of every foll 14th row until 6 inc rows have been completed. [125 (135: 143: 153) sts.] Rib 11 (15: 19: 23) rows straight, so ending with a WS row. **
Cast off loosely in rib.

FRONT

Work as back to **.
Lace panel (Also refer to chart on page 111.)
Cast off 26 (26: 30: 30) sts at beg of next 2 rows. [73 (83: 83: 93) sts.] Now patt as follows:

1st row: (RS) P1, skpo, rib to last 3 sts, k 2tog, p1.

2nd row: Beg and ending k1 and working each dec as p1tbl, rib to end.

3rd row: P1, skpo, rib 10, [k2tog, yo, k1tbl, yo, skpo, rib 5] 4 (5: 5: 6) times, k2tog, yo, k1tbl, yo, skpo, rib 10, k2tog, p1.

4th row: Rib 12, [p1tbl, p1, p1tbl, p1, p1tbl, rib 5] 4 (5: 5: 6) times, p1tbl, [p1, p1tbl] twice, rib 12.

5th row: P1, skpo, rib 8, [k2tog, yo, k3tbl, yo, skpo, p1, k1tbl, p1] 4 (5: 5: 6) times, k2tog, yo, k3tbl, yo, skpo, rib 8, k2tog, p1.

6th row: Patt sts as presented, working each dec as p1tbl and each yo as p1.

7th row: P1, skpo, rib 6, [k2tog, yo, k5tbl, yo, skpo, k1tbl] 4 (5: 5: 6) times, k2tog, yo, k5tbl, yo, skpo, rib 6, k2tog, p1.

8th row: As 6th row.

9th row: P1, skpo, rib 4, k2tog, yo, k1tbl, [k2tog, yo 3 times, sk2po, k1tbl, yo, sk2po, yo, k1tbl] 4 (5: 5: 6) times, k2tog, yo 3 times, sk2po, k1tbl, yo, skpo, rib 4, k2tog, p1.

10th row: As 6th row but working each triple yo as k1, p1, k1.

11th row: P1, skpo, rib 5, [yo, skpo, k3tbl, k2tog, yo, k3tbl] 4 (5: 5: 6) times, yo, skpo, k3tbl, k2tog, yo, rib 5, k2tog, p1.

12th row: As 6th row.

○ The lace stitch is explained with row-by-row instructions as well as with a chart, so if you haven't used a chart before you can, if necessary, refer from one to the other.

21st row: P1, k2tog, yo, k1tbl, [k2tog, yo 3 times, sk2po, k1tbl, yo, sk2po, yo, k1tbl] 4 (5: 5: 6) times, k2tog, yo 3 times, sk2po, k1tbl, yo, skpo, p1.

22nd row: As 20th row and working k1, p1, k1 into each triple yo.

23rd row: P1, k2tbl, [yo, skpo, k3tbl, k2tog, yo, k3tbl] 4 (5: 5: 6) times, yo, skpo, k3tbl, k2tog, yo, k2tbl, p1.

24th row: As 20th row.

25th row: P1, k3tbl, [yo, skpo, k1tbl, k2tog, yo, k5tbl] 4 (5: 5: 6) times, yo, skpo, k1tbl, k2tog, yo, k3tbl, p1.

26th row: As 20th row.

27th row: P1, k4tbl, [yo, sk2po, yo, k1tbl, k2tog, yo 3 times, sk2po, k1tbl] 4 (5: 5: 6) times, yo, sk2po, yo, k4tbl, p1.

28th row: As 22nd row.

29th row: P1, k2tbl, [k2tog, yo, k3tbl, yo, skpo, k3tbl] 4 (5: 5: 6) times, k2tog, yo, k3tbl, yo, skpo, k2tbl, p1.

30th row: As 20th row.

31st row: P1, k1tbl, [k2tog, yo, k5tbl, yo, skpo, k1tbl] 5 (6: 6: 7) times, p1.

20th–31st rows form lace patt. Rep 20th–31st rows 2 (2: 2: 3) times more, then patt 3 (9: 9: 3) more rows.

Next row: (RS) P1, * k1tbl, p1; rep from * to end.

Cont to rib as set for 10 rows. Cast off in rib.

TO MAKE UP

Join side seams. Turn rib at top of lace panel in half to the wrong side and catch down. Thread ribbon through this casing.

13th row: P1, skpo, rib 5, [yo, skpo, k1tbl, k2tog, yo, k5tbl] 4 (5: 5: 6) times, yo, skpo, k1tbl, k2tog, yo, rib 5, k2tog, p1.

14th row: As 6th row.

15th row: P1, skpo, rib 5, [yo, sk2po, yo, k1tbl, k2tog, yo 3 times, sk2po, k1tbl] 4 (5: 5: 6) times, yo, sk2po, yo, rib 5, k2tog, p1.

16th row: As 10th row.

17th row: P1, skpo, rib 2, [k2tog, yo, k3tbl, yo, skpo, k3tbl] 4 (5: 5: 6) times, k2tog, yo, k3tbl, yo, skpo, rib 2, k2tog, p1.

18th row: As 6th row.

19th row: P1, skpo, [k2tog, yo, k5tbl, yo, skpo, k1tbl] 4 (5: 5: 6) times, k2tog, yo, k5tbl, yo, skpo, k2tog, p1. [53 (63: 63: 73) sts.]

Now patt without side shaping:

20th row: (WS) K1, p1tbl to last st, k1.

Lace Panel Top Pattern

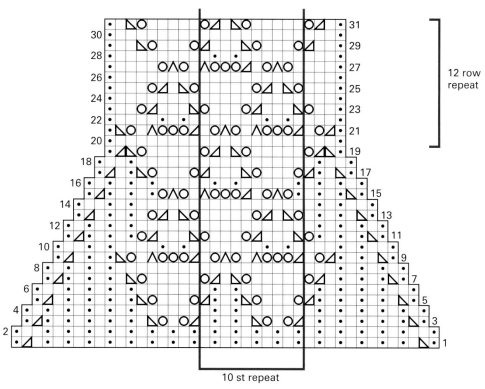

12 row repeat

10 st repeat

Key

☐ **K1tbl on RS rows, p1 tbl on WS rows ***

• **P1 on RS rows, k1 on WS rows**

O **yo**

◺ **k2tog**

◹ **skpo**

△ **sk2po**

NOTES

- Odd-numbered RS rows are read from right to left.
- Even-numbered WS rows are read from left to right.
- The exception to p1 tbl on WS rows is where a yo has been worked on the previous row. A single yo is worked p1 on the WS row and a triple yo is worked k1, p1, k1.

Black and White

Get that graphic look in dramatic black or laser-bright white. Luxuriate in the texture of a quick-to-knit fun fur bolero or create a film star effect with a super-furry hat and long lacy mitts. Knit the sweater equivalent of the ever useful little black dress with optional slits and slashes, go for a demure beaded lacy jumper, dare to bare your back in a laced-up corset top, or get a quick style fix with a sixties-look sequin and loop-knit bag.

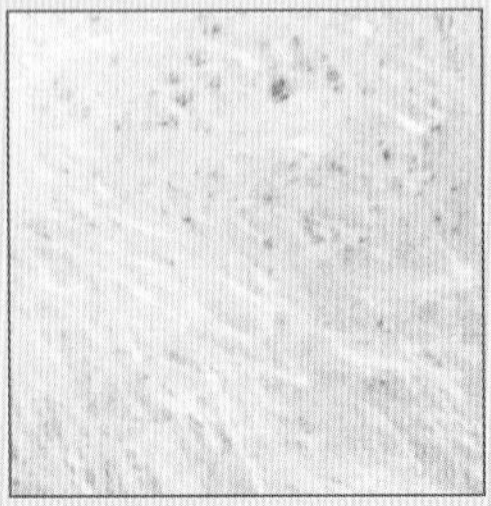

Enjoy cuddling into the luscious, thick pile of this little furry bolero.

Furry Bolero

EASY

MEASUREMENTS

To fit bust

in.	32	34	36	38	40	42
cm	81	86	91	97	102	107

Actual measurement across back

in.	16	17¼	18½	19¾	21¼	22½
cm	41	44	47	50	54	57

Actual length

in.	11	12¼	13	13¾	15	15¾
cm	28	31	33	35	38	40

Actual sleeve length

in.	8	8	8¼	8¼	8½	8½
cm	20	20	21	21	22	22

In the instructions, figures are given for the smallest size first; larger sizes follow in brackets. Where only one figure is given, this applies to all sizes.

MATERIALS

- 8 (8: 9: 9: 10: 10) × 1¾ oz. (50 g) balls of Sirdar Foxy in Ermine, 0417
- Pair of size 10½ (7 mm) knitting needles

TENSION

- 12¾ sts and 17 rows to 4 in. (10 cm) over st-st on size 10½ (7 mm) needles.

ABBREVIATIONS

See page 12.

BACK

Cast on 45 (49: 53: 57: 61: 65) sts.
Beg k row, st-st 2 rows.
3rd row: (RS) Kfb, k to last 2 sts, kfb, k1.
Beg p row, cont in st-st, inc one st as before at each end of every foll 4th row until a total of 4 inc rows has been completed. [53 (57: 61: 65: 69: 73) sts.]
Beg and ending p row, st-st 3 (5: 7: 9: 11: 13) rows straight.

- Counting rows can be difficult when working with a textured yarn, so use markers—either readymade ones or lengths of contrast yarn slipped between stitches.
- After making up, run the point of a needle along the seams to free any trapped pile and the seams will be completely invisible.

Shape Armholes

Cast off 3 (3: 4: 4: 5: 5) sts at beg of next 2 rows.

Next row: (RS) K1, k2tog, k to last 3 sts, skpo, k1.

Cont to dec in this way at each end of next 3 (4: 4: 5: 5: 6) RS rows. [39 (41: 43: 45: 47: 49) sts.]

Beg and ending p row, st-st 17 (17: 19: 19: 21: 21) rows straight.

Shape Neck

1st row: (RS) K11 (12: 13: 14: 15: 16) sts, turn. Leave rem sts on a spare needle and cont on these sts only for first side.

2nd row: P1, p 2 tog through back of loops, p to end.

3rd row: K to last 3 sts, skpo, k1.

Rep 2nd row, then cast off rem 8 (9: 10: 11: 12: 13) sts.

Next row: (RS) Rejoin yarn to inner end of rem sts, cast off center 17 sts, k to end.

2nd row: P to last 3 sts, p 2 tog, p1.

3rd row: K1, k2tog, k to end.

Rep 2nd row, then cast off rem 8 (9: 10: 11: 12: 13) sts.

LEFT FRONT

Cast on 12 (14: 16: 18: 20: 22) sts.

1st row: (RS) K to last 2 sts, kfb, k1.

2nd and WS rows: P.

3rd row: Kfb, k to last 2 sts, kfb, k1.

5th row: K to last 2 sts, kfb, k1.

** Cont to inc at front edge on every RS row and also at side edge on next and alternate RS rows until 15 rows have been completed. [24 (26: 28: 30: 32: 34] sts.] ***

Beg and ending p row, st-st 3 (5: 7: 9: 11: 13) rows straight.

Shape Armhole

Cast off 3 (3: 4: 4: 5: 5) sts at beg of next row.

P one row.

Next row: (RS) K1, k2tog, k to end.

Cont to dec in this way at beg of next 3 (4: 4: 5: 5: 6) RS rows. [17 (18: 19: 20: 21: 22) sts.]

P one row.

Shape Front Edge

1st row: (RS) K to last 3 sts, skpo, k1.

Cont to dec in this way at end of next 8 RS rows. [8 (9: 10: 11: 12: 13) sts.]

Beg and ending p row, st-st 3 (3: 5: 5: 7: 7) rows straight.

Cast off.

RIGHT FRONT

Cast on 12 (14: 16: 18: 20: 22) sts.

1st row: (RS) Kfb, k to end.

2nd and WS rows: P.

3rd row: Kfb, k to last 2 sts, kfb, k1.

5th row: Kfb, k to end.

Cont as given for left front from ** to ***.

Beg p row and ending k row, st-st 4 (6: 8: 10: 12: 14) rows straight.

Shape Armhole

Cast off 3 (3: 4: 4: 5: 5) sts at beg of next row.

Next row: (RS) K to last 3 sts, skpo, k1.

Cont to dec in this way at end of next 3 (4: 4: 5: 5: 6) RS rows. [17 (18: 19: 20: 21: 22) sts.]

P one row.

Shape Front Edge

1st row: (RS) K1, k2tog, k to end.

Cont to dec in this way at beg of next 8 RS
  rows. [8 (9: 10: 11: 12: 13) sts.]

Beg and ending p row, st-st 3 (3: 5: 5: 7: 7)
  rows straight.

Cast off.

SLEEVES

Cast on 32 (34: 37: 39: 42: 44) sts.

Beg k row, st-st 4 (4: 6: 6: 8: 8) rows.

Next row: (RS) Kfb, k to last 2 sts, kfb, k1.

Cont to inc in this way on every foll 6th row
  until there are 42 (44: 47: 49: 52: 54) sts.

Beg and ending p row, st-st 5 rows straight.

Shape Top

Cast off 3 (3: 4: 4: 5: 5) sts at beg of next 2
  rows.

Next row: (RS) K1, k2tog, k to last 3 sts, skpo,
  k1.

Cont to dec in this way at each end of next 3
  (4: 4: 5: 5: 6) RS rows. [28 (28: 29: 29: 30: 30)
  sts.]

Dec 1 st at each end of every foll 4th row 3
  times. [22 (22: 23: 23: 24: 24) sts.]

Dec 1 st at each end of next 3 rows as for
  back neck shaping.

Cast off rem 16 (16: 17: 17: 18: 18) sts.

TO MAKE UP

Join shoulder seams. Set in sleeves. Join side
  and sleeve seams.

This sexy sweater is made from simple, shaped strips of rolled edge, stocking stitch, with gaps left open as big as you dare when joining the seams.

Slits and Slashes Sweater

EASY

MEASUREMENTS

Stretches to fit bust

in.	32	34	36	38	40	42
cm	81	86	91	97	102	107

Actual bust

in.	31½	33½	36	38	40¼	42¾
cm	80	85.5	91	97	102.5	108.5

Actual length

in.	23	23¾	24¼	24¾	25¼	26
cm	58.5	60.5	61.5	63	64	66

Actual sleeve length

in.	18
cm	46

In the instructions, figures are given for the smallest size first; larger sizes follow in brackets. Where only one figure is given, this applies to all sizes.

MATERIALS

- 5 (6: 6: 7: 7: 8) × 1¾ oz. (50 g) balls of Sirdar Town and Country 4ply in Black, shade 151
- Pair of size 3 (3.25 mm) knitting needles

TENSION

- 28 sts and 36 rows to 4 in. (10 cm) over st-st on size 3 (3.25 mm) needles. Change needle size if necessary to obtain this tension.

ABBREVIATIONS

- **rev** – reverse
- **[ ]** – work instructions in square brackets as directed

See also page 12.

NOTES

- The back and front are each knitted in two halves then joined leaving gaps.
- The sleeve is worked in the opposite way to the usual construction, so the inside arm increases—normally made on each side of the seam—are in the center, and the seam which will be joined with gaps runs up the outer arm.

- Mark each shaping with a loop of contrast smooth thread. Use the threads to help match the pieces when sewing up.
- You can join as much or as little of each of the seams as you wish.
- Pin the back and front pieces together before sewing and try on the sweater to make sure you are happy with the spacing of the gaps in the seams. Take the sweater off and check that the spacing is even before sewing.

Dec in same way as before at beg of next row and on 10 (11: 12: 13: 14: 15) foll RS rows. [51 (54: 57: 60: 63: 66) sts.]
Work 49 (51: 53: 55: 57: 59) rows. Cast off.

LEFT BACK

Work as given for right back to **.
Dec row: (RS) P3, k to last 7 sts, skpo, k2, p3.
Cont in st-st with rev st-st at each side, dec in this way at end of 5 foll 6th rows. [56 (60: 64: 68: 72: 76) sts.]
Work 15 rows.
Inc row: (RS) P3, k to last 6 sts, kfb, k2, p3.
Cont in st-st with rev st-st at each side, inc in this way at end of 5 foll 6th rows. [62 (66: 70: 74: 78: 82) sts.]
Work 33 (35: 35: 37: 37: 39) rows.

Shape Armhole

Dec in same way as before at end of next row and on 10 (11: 12: 13: 14: 15) foll RS rows. [51 (54: 57: 60: 63: 66) sts.]
Work 49 (51: 53: 55: 57: 59) rows. Cast off.

LEFT FRONT

Work as given for right back.

RIGHT FRONT

Work as given for left back.

RIGHT BACK

Cast on 62 (66: 70: 74: 78: 82) sts.
1st row: (RS) P3, k to last 3 sts, p3.
2nd row: K3, p to last 3 sts, k3.
These 2 rows form st-st with 3 sts in rev st-st at each side. Work 30 more rows **.
Dec row: (RS) P3, k2, k2tog, k to last 3 sts, p3.
Cont in st-st with rev st-st at each side, dec in this way at beg of 5 foll 6th rows. [56 (60: 64: 68: 72: 76) sts.]
Work 15 rows.
Inc row: (RS) P3, k1, kfb, k to last 3 sts, p3.
Cont in st-st with rev st-st at each side, inc in this way at beg of 5 foll 6th rows. [62 (66: 70: 74: 78: 82) sts.]
Work 33 (35: 35: 37: 37: 39) rows.

SLEEVES

Cast on 60 (62: 64: 66: 68: 70) sts.

1st row: (RS) P3, k24 (25: 26: 27: 28: 29), p6, k24 (25: 26: 27: 28: 29), p3.

2nd row: K3, p24 (25: 26: 27: 28: 29), k6, p24 (25: 26: 27: 28: 29), k3.

These 2 rows form st-st with 3 sts in rev st-st at each side and 6 sts in rev st-st at center. Work 38 (30: 30: 22: 22: 14) more rows.

Inc row: (RS) P3, k until 3 sts before 6 sts at center, kfb, k2, p6, k1, kfb, k to last 3 sts, p3.

Cont inc in this way at each side of center 6 sts on 12 (13: 14: 15: 16: 17) foll 8th rows. [86 (90: 94: 98: 102: 106) sts.]

Work 29 (29: 21: 21: 13: 13) rows straight.

Shape Top

1st row: (RS) P3, k33 (35: 37: 39: 41: 43), skpo, k2, p3, turn and complete 1st side on these 42 (44: 46: 48: 50: 52) sts.

Noting that there will be one less k st before dec each time, dec in this way at end of next 10 (11: 12: 13: 14: 15) RS rows. [32 (33: 34: 35: 36: 37) sts.] Work 7 rows straight.

Dec as before at end of next 21 (22: 23: 24: 25: 26) RS rows. [11 sts.]

Work 1 row. Cast off.

With RS facing, join yarn for 2nd side.

1st row: (RS) P3, k2, k2tog, k to last 3 sts, p3. [42 (44: 46: 48: 50: 52) sts.]

Dec in this way at beg of next 10 (11: 12: 13: 14: 15) RS rows. [32 (33: 34: 35: 36: 37) sts.]

Work 7 rows straight.

Dec as before at beg of next 21 (22: 23: 24: 25: 26) RS rows. [11 sts.]

Work 1 row. Cast off.

TO MAKE UP

Press all pieces according to ball band.

Leaving six gaps open, mark position to join left and right back pieces along straight edges. With WS facing, using mattress stitch and omitting rolled edge sts to bring the RS of st-st together, join approximately 6 rows at lower edge, between gaps and at top of center back seam. Marking positions for 4 gaps and leaving the top part of each piece free for collar, join center front seam in the same way. Join 19 (20: 21: 22: 23: 24) sts of back and front for each shoulder. Ending at start of armhole shaping, join side seams in the same way as the front. Join cast-off edges at sleeve top. Spacing gaps evenly, join straight edges of sleeves in the same way as back. Set in sleeves.

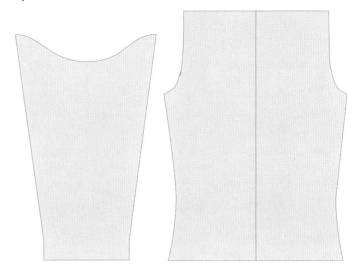

Dare to bare your back in this curvy little top with dramatic lace-up detail.

Corset Top

MEASUREMENTS

To fit bust

in.	32	34	36	38
cm	81	86	91	97

Actual front width at bust

in.	15¾	16¾	17¾	19
cm	40	42.5	45	48

Actual length

in.	17¾	18	18½	19
cm	45	46	47	48

In the instructions, figures are given for the smallest size first; larger sizes follow in brackets. Where only one figure is given, this applies to all sizes.

MATERIALS

- 4 (4: 5: 5) × 1¾ oz. (50 g) balls of Debbie Bliss Cathay in Black, shade 01
- Pair of size 5 (3.75 mm) knitting needles
- Size 5 (3.75 mm) circular needle, 39½ in. (100 cm) long
- 3¼ yd. (3 m) narrow black cord

TENSION

- 22 sts and 30 rows to 4 in. (10 cm) over st-st on size 5 (3.75 mm) needles. Change needle size if necessary to obtain this tension.

ABBREVIATIONS

- **ssp** – slip the first st knitwise, then the 2nd st, return sts to left needle noting that they now face the opposite way to the other sts, take right needle behind and through 2nd, then first st to p2tog
- **[ ]** – work instructions in square brackets as directed

See also page 12.

NOTE

- You can use straight needles or the circular needle to work the pieces of the top but you will need to use the circular needle for the picot edging because of the amount of stitches.

- Because the back laces up, it is not possible to give an actual bust measurement. If you are not sure which size to make, measure around your bust, divide the amount in half and make the nearest size. If in doubt, go for a slightly smaller, rather than larger size as the knitting will stretch to fit.
- If you are not familiar with working ssp, practise it on your sample swatch. It is easy to do and you'll find that it gives the exact opposite of p2tog, so the stitches at the shaped edges of the front are a mirror image.

FRONT

Cast on 78 (84: 90: 96) sts. Beg k row, st-st 4 rows.

Dec row: (RS) K3, k2tog, k to last 5 sts, skpo, k3.

Cont in st-st, dec in this way at each end of 3 foll 4th rows. [70 (76: 82: 88) sts.] St-st 5 rows.

Inc row: (RS) K2, kfb, k to last 4 sts, kfb, k3.

Cont in st-st, inc in this way at each end of 9 foll 6th rows. [90 (96: 102: 108) sts.]

St-st 5 (5: 7: 7) rows.

Shape Neck and Armholes

1st row: (RS) K42 (45: 48: 51), skpo, k1, turn and complete left side on these 44 (47: 50: 53) sts, leaving 45 (48: 51: 54) sts for right side.

2nd row: P1, ssp, p to end.

3rd row: Cast off 4 (5: 5: 6) sts, k to last 3 sts, skpo, k1. [38 (40: 43: 45) sts.]

4th row: P1, ssp, p to end.

5th row: K1, k2tog, k to last 3 sts, skpo, k1.

Work 4th and 5th rows 5 (6: 7: 8) more times. [20 (19: 19: 18) sts.] Dec as before at neck edge only on next 9 (7: 6: 4) rows. [11 (12: 13: 14) sts.] St-st 30 (32: 33: 35) rows. Cast off.

With RS facing, join yarn to remaining 45 (48: 51: 54) sts for right side.

1st row: (RS) K1, k2tog, k to end.

2nd row: P to last 3 sts, p2tog, p1.

3rd row: As 1st.

4th row: Cast off 4 (5: 5: 6) sts, p to last 3 sts, p2tog, p1. [37 (39: 42: 44) sts.]

5th row: K1, k2tog, k to last 3 sts skpo, k1.

6th row: P to last 3 sts, p2tog, p1.

Work 5th and 6th rows 5 (6: 7: 8) more times. [19 (18: 18: 17) sts.]

Dec as before at neck edge only on next 8 (6: 5: 3) rows. [11 (12: 13: 14) sts.]

St-st 30 (32: 33: 35) rows. Cast off.

RIGHT BACK

Cast on 15 (18: 20: 23) sts. Beg k, st-st 4 rows.

Dec row: (RS) K3, k2tog, k to end.

Cont in st-st, dec in this way at beg of 3 foll 4th rows. [11 (14: 16: 19) sts.] St-st 5 rows.

Inc row: (RS) K2, kfb, k to end.

Cont in st-st, inc in this way at beg of 9 foll 6th rows. [21 (24: 26: 29) sts.]

St-st 7 (7: 9: 9) rows.

Shape Armhole

Cast off 4 (5: 5: 6) sts at beg of next row.

P 1 row.

Dec row: (RS) K1, k2tog, k to end.

○ When shaping the top of the sleeve, slip the first stitch of each cast-off group for a smoother line.
○ The cord is threaded through the picot points of the edging so you can adjust the spacing and start higher up or lower down the back to get the fit that's best for you.

Cont in st-st, dec in this way at beg of next 5 (6: 7: 8) RS rows. [11 (12: 13: 14) sts.] St-st 39 rows. Cast off.

LEFT BACK

Cast on 15 (18: 20: 23) sts. Beg k, st-st 4 rows.
Dec row: (RS) K to last 5 sts, skpo, k3.
Cont in st-st, dec in this way at end of 3 foll 4th rows. [11 (14: 16: 19) sts.] St-st 5 rows.
Inc row: (RS) K to last 4 sts, kfb, k3.
Cont in st-st, inc in this way at end of 9 foll 6th rows. [21 (24: 26: 29) sts.] St-st 8 (8: 10: 10) rows.

Shape Armhole

Cast off 4 (5: 5: 6) sts at beg of next row.
Dec row: (RS) K to last 3 sts, skpo, k1.
Cont in st-st, dec in this way at end of next 5 (6: 7: 8) RS rows. [11 (12: 13: 14) sts.] St-st 39 rows. Cast off.

SLEEVES

Cast on 68 (72: 74: 78) sts. Beg k, st-st 2 rows.

Shape Top

Cast off 4 (5: 5: 6) sts at beg of next 2 rows.
Dec row: (RS) K1, k2tog, k to last 3 sts, skpo, k1.
Cont in st-st, dec in this way at each end of next 13 (14: 15: 16) RS rows. [32 sts.] P 1 row.
[Cast off 2 sts at beg and work skpo at end of next row. Cast off 2 sts at beg and work p2tog at end of foll row] 3 times. 14 sts. Cast off.

right front neck shaping, 18 (21: 23: 25) sts to shoulder and 97 (100: 103: 106) sts down right back. [279 (291: 303: 315) sts.] K 1 row.

Picot row: (RS) K2, cast off one st, [return st to left needle, cast on 2 sts, cast off 2 sts, k2tog, cast off one st, k1, cast off one st] to end, ending last repeat k1, cast off one st, fasten off.

Sleeve Edgings

K up 69 (72: 75: 78) sts along cast-on edge. Complete as given for back and neck edging.

Lower Edging

Set in sleeves. Join side and sleeve seams. K up 13 (16: 19: 22) sts along lower right back edge, 76 (82: 88: 94) sts along front edge and 13 (16: 19: 22) sts along left back edge. [102 (114: 126: 138) sts.]

Complete as given for back and neck edging. Thread lace through the holes in the picot edge at each side of the back. Adjust lacing to fit and tie ends.

TO MAKE UP

Back and Neck Edging

Join shoulders. Using circular needle, k up 97 (100: 103: 106) sts up left back. 18 (21: 23: 25) sts down left front neck to start of shaping, 24 (24: 25: 26) sts to center, one st from between center 2 sts, 24 (24: 25: 26) sts up

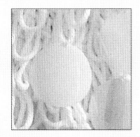

Sling this sixties-style bag over your shoulder for instant retro chic.

Sequin Shoulder Bag

EASY

MEASUREMENTS

9 in. (23 cm) wide × 6.75 in. (17 cm) deep

MATERIALS

- 2 × 3½ oz. (100 g) balls of Sirdar Pure Cotton in White, 029
- Pair each of size 3 (3.25 mm) and size 5 (3.75 mm) knitting needles
- Oval paillette sequins
- Fine sewing needle and white sewing thread
- Two split rings

ABBREVIATIONS

- **lp1** – make a loop: k the next st but do not slip it off the needle; bring the yarn to the front between the needles, take it under then over your left thumb and back between the needles; k the st on left-hand needle again and slip it off in the usual way then pass the next st on the right-hand needle over it. For an illustration see page 21.
- **g-st** – garter stitch: k every row

See also page 12.

BACK

Using size 5 (3.75 mm) needles, cast on 43 sts.
1st row: (RS) K1, * lp1, k1; rep from * to end.

2nd row: K1, p41, k1.
3rd row: K2, * lp1, k1; rep from * to last st, k1.
4th row: As 2nd row.
These 4 rows form pattern. Rep 1st–4th rows 9 times more, then work first row again, so ending with a RS row.
Change to size 3 (3.25 mm) needles and g-st 4 rows.
Cast off knitwise.

FRONT

As back.

HANDLE

Using size 3 (3.25 mm) needles, cast on 205 sts.
G-st 3 rows.
Cast off knitwise.

TO MAKE UP

Placing front on back, wrong sides together, use the knitting yarn to back stitch side and base seams, one stitch in from edge. With sewing thread randomly stitch paillettes to ends of loops, scattering them more thinly toward the top of the bag.
Insert a split ring through the front and back of the bag near each top corner. Use the knitting yarn to attach each end of the handle to a split ring, oversewing around the ring.

Ultra long hair yarn makes this simple hat look very dramatic. Wear it plain or add decoration for a special occasion.

Faux Fur Hat

EASY

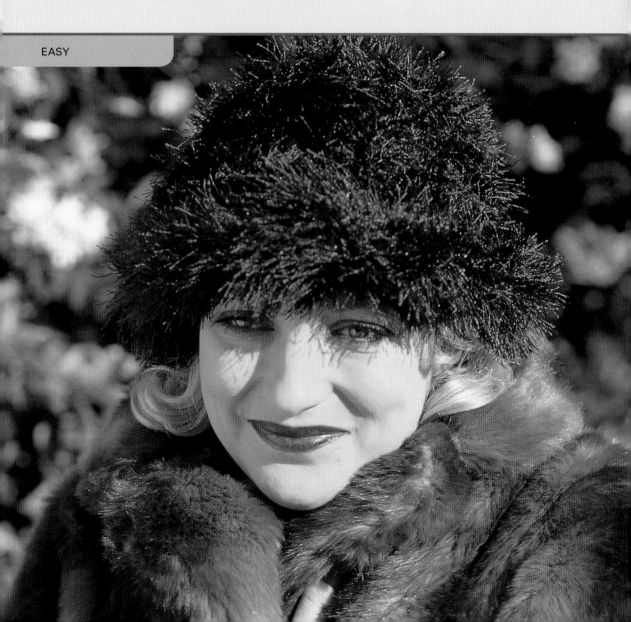

MEASUREMENTS

Actual measurement around head

in.   22

cm 56

MATERIALS

- 3 x 1¾ oz. (50 g) balls of Sirdar Foxy in Beaver, shade 0148
- Pair of size 10½ (7 mm) knitting needles

TENSION

- 12½ sts and 17 rows to 4 in. (10 cm) over st-st on size 10½ (7 mm) needles. Change needle size if necessary to obtain this tension.

ABBREVIATIONS

- **sk2po** – slip one knitwise, k2tog, pass slipped st over
- **[ ]** – work instructions in square brackets as directed

See also page 12.

NOTES

- If you'd rather knit to length for the brim, lay the work flat and make sure that it measures 8 in. (20 cm) wide before measuring the length. At the correct tension the 77 rows will measure 17¾ in. (45 cm) but this will stretch to measure 22 in. (56 cm).
- When picking up the stitches for the crown, skip approximately every 11th row-end.

BRIM

Cast on 25 sts. Beg k row, st-st 77 rows. Cast off.

CROWN

With WS facing, k up 71 sts along one long edge of the brim.

Beg p row, st-st 7 rows.

Shape Top

1st dec row: (RS) K1, [k2tog, k5, skpo, k1] 7 times. [57 sts.] P 1 row.

2nd dec row: K1, [k2tog, k3, skpo, k1] 7 times. [43 sts.] P 1 row.

3rd dec row: K1, [k2tog, k1, skpo, k1] 7 times. [29 sts.] P 1 row.

4th dec row: K1, [s2kpo, k1] 7 times. [15 sts.] P 1 row.

5th dec row: K1, [k2tog] 7 times. [8 sts.] Leaving a long end, cut yarn.

TO MAKE UP

Thread end through sts at top of crown, draw up and secure. Join back seam, reversing seam for rolled up brim.

These pretty fingerless mitts are just simple, lacy tubes that are knitted in the round, so there are no seams and very little making up!

Lacy Fingerless Mitts

- If you want longer mitts, weigh the remaining yarn while knitting the first mitt and cast off when almost 1 oz. (25 g) of yarn has been used. There should then be enough yarn to make the second mitt the same length.
- The instructions are written for a set of 4 double-pointed needles. If you have a set of 5 needles, cast on 10 sts on each of the first 3 needles and 12 sts on the 4th needle, making a total of 42 sts.
- Why work with the wrong side facing? Because yarn over, p2tog is easier to work than yarn over, k2tog, try it and see!

MEASUREMENTS

Stretches to fit around hand

in.	9½
cm	24

Stretches to length

in.	15
cm	38

Actual measurement around glove

in.	18
cm	20

Actual length

in.	10½
cm	27

MATERIALS

- 1¾ oz. (50 g) ball of Sirdar Town and Country 4ply in Black, 151
- Set of size 3 (3.25 mm) double-pointed knitting needles
- 19½ in. (50 cm) of narrow black lacy lingerie elastic
- Black sewing thread and sharp needle

TENSION

- 21 sts and 39 rows to 4 in. (10 cm) over lacy patt in the round, not stretched, on size 3 (3.25 mm) needles. Change needle size if necessary to obtain this tension.

ABBREVIATIONS

- [ ] – work instructions in square brackets asdirected

See also page 12.

NOTE

- When joining to make a round, check that the stitches are not twisted on the needles.

FIRST MITT

Cast on 14 sts on each of 3 needles. [42 sts.] Join in a round. K 1 round.

Next round: (WS) [Yo, p2tog] to end.

This round forms lacy patt. Work 105 more rounds. K 2 rounds.

Cast off round: K1, yo, cast off one st, [k1, cast off one st, yo, cast off one st] to end. Fasten off.

SECOND MITT

Work as given for first mitt.

TO MAKE UP

Turn mitts inside out so right side faces. Try on, mark position, and stitch to make thumbholes in cast-off edges. Darn in ends. Sew lacy elastic around cast-off edges.

This shapely jumper has a subtle lace pattern outlined with beads between the leafy panels.

Beaded Lacy Jumper

MEASUREMENTS

To fit bust

in.	32	34	36	38	40	42	44	46
cm	81	86	91	97	102	107	112	117

Actual bust

in.	34½	36½	38	39¾	41½	43	45	46½
cm	88	92.5	97	101	105.5	109.5	114	118

Actual length

in.	22	22	23¼	23¼	25¼	25¼	26¼	26¼
cm	56	56	59	59	64	64	67	67

Actual sleeve length

in.	18	18	18	18	19	19	19	19
cm	45.5	45.5	45.5	45.5	48	48	48	48

In the instructions, figures are given for the smallest size first; larger sizes follow in brackets. Where only one figure is given, this applies to all sizes.

MATERIALS

- 4 (4: 4: 5: 5: 5: 6: 6) × 3½ oz. (100 g) balls of Sirdar Pure Cotton 4ply in Black, 041
- Pair of size 3 (3.25 mm) knitting needles
- Size 3 (3.25 mm) circular needle, 23½ in. (60 cm) long
- 17½ oz. (500 g) (approximately 5,300) rocaille glass beads

TENSION

- 28 sts to 4 in. (10 cm) over st-st, 24 sts measure 3⅛ in. (8 cm), 30 rows to 4 in. (10 cm) over beaded lace patt on size 3 (3.25 mm) needles. Change needle size if necessary to obtain these tensions.

ABBREVIATIONS

- **B** – bring a bead up close to work
- **sk2po** – slip one knitwise, k2tog, pass slipped st over
- **ssk and pass** – slip the first st knitwise, then the 2nd, return sts to left needle noting that they now face the opposite way and k2tog, slip st just made from right to left needle, lift 2nd st on left needle over first, return st to right needle
- **[ ]** – work instructions in square brackets as directed

See also page 12.

NOTES

- Work with beaded yarn throughout. Thread as many beads as is practical on

- The beads used for this design are metallic-coated glass beads. Although there will be some beads left over in the smaller sizes, a 17½ oz. (500 g) pack (approximately 5,300 beads) is recommended for all sizes as buying beads in smaller amounts can work out more expensive. This will also allow for some beads being malformed or with holes too small to thread on to the yarn.
- Because the beads hang between stitches, they do not need to be included in the stitch counts.

to yarn before starting to knit. When there are not enough beads left to complete a row, cut yarn at the beginning of a row, thread on more beads and rejoin yarn. Never join in new yarn or add beads during a row.
- Cast on by the knitting-off-the-thumb method (see pages 14–15).

BACK

Sliding a bead up close between each st, cast on 126 (126: 130: 136: 140: 140: 146: 150) sts.

1st and every WS row: P2 (2: 4: 7: 9: 9: 12: 14), [k2, p10] to last 4 (4: 6: 9: 11: 11: 14: 16) sts, k2, p2 (2: 4: 7: 9: 9: 12: 14).

2nd row: (RS) K2 (2: 4: 7: 9: 9: 12: 14), [p1, B, p1, k6, ssk and pass, yo, k1, yo, p1, B, p1, yo, k1, yo, sk2po, k6] to last 4 (4: 6: 9: 11: 11: 14: 16) sts, p1, B, p1, k2 (2: 4: 7: 9: 9: 12: 14).

4th row: K2 (2: 4: 7: 9: 9: 12: 14), * p1, B, p1, k4, ssk and pass, [k1, yo] twice, k1, p1, B, p1, [k1, yo] twice, k1, sk2po, k4, rep from * to last 4 (4: 6: 9: 11: 11: 14: 16) sts, p1, B, p1, k2 (2: 4: 7: 9: 9: 12: 14).

6th row: K2 (2: 4: 7: 9: 9: 12: 14), [p1, B, p1, k2, ssk and pass, k2, yo, k1, yo, k2, p1, B, p1, k2, yo, k1, yo, k2, sk2po, k2] to last 4 (4: 6: 9: 11: 11: 14: 16) sts, p1, B, p1, k2 (2: 4: 7: 9: 9: 12: 14).

8th row: K2 (2: 4: 7: 9: 9: 12: 14), [p1, B, p1, ssk and pass, k3, yo, k1, yo, k3, p1, B, p1, k3, yo, k1, yo, k3, sk2po] to last 4 (4: 6: 9: 11: 11: 14: 16) sts, p1, B, p1, k2 (2: 4: 7: 9: 9: 12: 14).

These 8 rows form the beaded lace patt.

Cont in patt, work 49 (49: 41: 41: 41: 25: 25: 17) more rows.

Inc row: (RS) Kfb, patt to last 2 sts, kfb, k1.

- Note that when decreasing for the armhole and top of sleeve, to keep the pattern correct on the smaller sizes it will be necessary to work k4tog at the beginning and slip one, k3tog, pass slipped stitch over at the end when the double decrease in the pattern reaches the edges.
- Although metallic beads are used for the jumper in the picture, you can use any beads you like as long as they have a hole that is large enough to thread them onto the yarn.
- Although the cotton yarn can be machine washed, to protect the beads it's best to turn the jumper inside out and hand wash it. If you want to spin the jumper in a machine to remove excess water, put it in a washing bag or a pillowcase.

Taking incs into st-st at each side, cont in patt, inc in this way at each end of 2 (5: 6: 6: 7: 10: 10: 11) foll 16th (8th: 8th: 8th: 8th: 8th: 8th: 8th) rows. [132 (138: 144: 150: 156: 162: 168: 174) sts.]
Patt 23 (15: 15: 15: 15: 7: 7: 7) rows.

Shape Armholes

Cast off 3 (6: 6: 7: 7: 8: 9: 12) sts at beg of next 2 rows.
Keeping patt correct for smaller sizes, dec one st at each end of next 13 RS rows. [100 (100: 106: 110: 116: 120: 124: 124) sts **.]
Taking sts at each side of patt into st-st, patt 29 (29: 37: 37: 45: 45: 53: 53) rows. Cast off.

FRONT

Work as given for back to **.
Patt 20 (20: 28: 28: 36: 36: 44: 44) rows.

Shape Neck

Next row: (WS) P1(1: 4: 6: 9: 0: 1: 1) , k2 (2: 2: 2: 2: 1: 2: 2), [p10, k2] 1 (1: 1: 1: 1: 2: 2: 2) times, p4, turn and complete right side on these 19 (19: 22: 24: 27: 29: 31: 31) sts.
Dec row: (RS) K2tog, patt to end.
Cont in patt, dec in this way at beg of next 2 RS rows. [16 (16: 19: 21: 24: 26: 28: 28) sts.]
Patt 3 rows. Cast off.
With WS facing, leave center 62 sts on a holder, patt to end. [19 (19: 22: 24: 27: 29: 31: 31) sts.]
Dec row: (RS) Patt to last 2 sts, skpo.

- If you want to make the jumper without the beads, simply omit all the beads for a pretty, lacy, daytime knit. But without the weight of the beads, the row tension could be tighter, so be prepared to add more rows, if necessary, to get the length.
- Black is the classic winter party color, for a subtle effect you could use black glass instead of metallic beads. Other combinations of yarn and bead color could also work well, such as pastel and silver for a summer party or white and pearly beads for a wedding.

Cont in patt, dec in this way at end of next 2 RS rows. [16 (16: 19: 21: 24: 26: 28: 28) sts.] Patt 3 rows. Cast off.

SLEEVES

Sliding a bead up close between each st, cast on 78 (78: 82: 88: 92: 92: 98: 102) sts. Work in patt as given for back for 81 (81: 73: 73: 73: 57: 57: 49) rows.

Inc in same way as back at each end of next row and on 2 (5: 6: 6: 7: 10: 10: 11) foll 16th (8th: 8th: 8th: 8th: 8th: 8th: 8th) rows. [84 (90: 96: 102: 108: 114: 120: 126) sts]

Patt 23 (15: 15: 15: 15: 7: 7: 7) rows.

Shape Top

Cast off 3 (6: 6: 7: 7: 8: 9: 12) sts at beg of next 2 rows. Keeping patt correct, dec one st at

each end of next row and on foll 14 (14: 17: 19: 22: 24: 26: 26) RS rows. [48 sts.]

Patt 1 row. Cast off 2 sts at beg and dec one st at end of next 8 rows. [24 sts.] Cast off.

NECK EDGING

Matching sts, join shoulders. Using circular needle, k up 68 sts across back neck and 8 sts down left front neck, patt 62 sts from holder, k up 8 sts up right front neck. [146 sts.] Sliding a bead up close between sts each time, cast off loosely purlwise.

TO MAKE UP

Laying pieces out with WS facing and using a pressing cloth to protect the beads, press according to ball band to open out the lace pattern. Set in sleeves. Join side and sleeve seams.

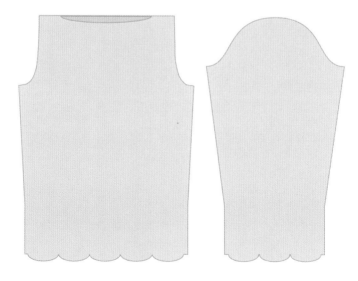

Suppliers

All suppliers listed ship internationally unless otherwise stated.

A.C. Moore Arts & Crafts
www.acmoore.com
This US-based arts and crafts supply chain store sells knitting goods, including yarn, needles, beads, and notions. The website does not offer shipping on their products, internationally or domestically.

Amazon
www.amazon.com
As one of the world's largest online retailers, Amazon is a definite go-to source for purchasing anything knitting-related.

Black Sheep Wools
wwwblacksheepwools.com
A family-owned business, Black Sheep Wools sells yarn, patterns, books, and accessories.

Debbie Bliss
www.debbieblissonline.com
For all your Debbie Bliss brand needs, why not go straight to the source? In addition to their beand of speciality yarn, Debbie Bliss also sells knitting patterns, both free and for a small fee.

Ebay
www.ebay.com.com
For those hard-to-find yarn brands or colors, it might be best to turn to Ebay. You can also use this site to find just about any type of notion needed for knitting.

Jimmy Beans Wool
www.jimmybeanswool.com
This retailer sells yarn, needles, patterns, kits, and notions.

Joann
www.joann.com
This crafty chain retailer is an excellent source for knitting supplies, yarn, beads, sequins, and trimmings. International shipping is not available.

Knit-n-Crochet
www.knit-n-crochet.com
This retailer sells a wide variety of specialty yarns, kits, and knitting and crochet supplies.

Love Knitting
www.loveknitting.com
Love Knitting offers a multitude of brands, patterns, tools, kits, and how-to tutorials for knitting techiniques.

Michaels
www.michaels.com
Michaels is a one-stop shop for a variety of arts and crafts supplies, including knitting accessories, yarn, beads, sequins, and trimmings. International shipping is not available.

WEBS
www.yarn.com
This family-owned business sells an assortment of yarn brands, patterns, kits, and knitting essentials.

Index

Acknowledgements

Many thanks to Rosemary Wilkinson for giving us the opportunity to work together again. Thanks also to Clare Hubbard and everyone else involved in making this book.

For the inspirational yarns, thanks to: Debbie Bliss and all at Designer Yarns; Mike Cole and all at Elle Yarns; Kate Buller and all at Rowan and Jaeger; David Rawson and all at Sirdar.

For help with the knitting, thanks to: Brenda Bostock, Sally Buss, Helen Fraser, Gwen Radford, Jean Trehane, and Hilary Underwood.

Finally, but most important of all, thank you to Sue Horan for checking the instructions.